PRAISE ▌
Home Is Here

"*Home Is Here* is a pioneering book and a must-read for all students and teachers of Buddhism. These days, inclusivity in sangha requires that the Buddhist world strengthen and clarify our understanding of self, society, racism and antiracism, and dharma. Antiracism is neither an ad-hoc addition to Buddhism nor are the ancient teachings a ready-made or obvious response to the complexities of racism in the contemporary world. This book is a jewel and essence of Reverend Liên's teachings on dharma and race, evolved over her many years of teaching.

Home Is Here is about wholeness and Buddhist truth. Finding wholeness—the place of spiritual, physical, and emotional belonging—can be challenging in the midst of individual and societal turmoil. The work of antiracism carries with it the weight of history and individual experience. Nonetheless, Reverend Liên's practices and inquiries, which she has been honing and cultivating for many years, offer possibilities of resilience and renewal. This book is her gift to us, born of a long practice life, honed in the grit of hurt and healing, and deeply immersed in dharma. It is a book for everyone."

> —REV. DANA TAKAGI, professor emerita of sociology at Rachel Carson College, UCS

"Having known Reverend Shutt for more than twenty years, it gives me an inspired joy that she has offered a path . . . a journey . . . a practice, in the broadest sense of the word, through the suffering of oppression and supremacy that is endemic in our world. In that way, she has shown that the suffering, the way through the suffering, and the teachings are universal—and how to use our specific social locations for the benefit of the greater whole, without being used by them."

> —LARRY YANG, author of *Awakening Together*

"*Home Is Here* is not only a book to be read but a set of principles to be enacted. In this wonderful Buddhist manifesto for change, Rev. Liên Shutt calls us all into integrity and insists we examine thoroughly the oppressive systems that harm all of humanity. Sharing her lived experience as an Asian American lesbian and ordained Zen teacher, she calls us into a deep investigation of our actions as Buddhist and non-Buddhist, not simply for awareness or awakening but for actual transformation and healing among us. She calls us into being stewards of all life as an act of wholeness in the midst of collective suffering. Finally, she reminds us that oppressive acts are not one-time events but rather results of a prolonged and ingrained consciousness of believing one kind of person is more superior than another. A must for all those who seek true liberation and are willing to do the work."

—ZENJU EARTHLYN MANUEL, author of *The Way of Tenderness*, *The Deepest Peace*, and *The Shamanic Bones of Zen*

"*Home Is Here* is like a good Zen retreat, in which the bottom drops out of the trap of habitual perceptions and reactions, freeing us from suffering. Accessible, grounded and vital, Liên Shutt's work interweaves how-to's of the Buddha Way with her own rich experience as one who sets forth in the forbidding landscape of racism to reach—her and our—true home."

—SHOSAN VICTORIA AUSTIN, contributor to *The Hidden Lamp*

"We practice to 'come home' to the home that's already here [and to wholeness], the author of *Home Is Here*, T. Liên Shutt, says. In this warm and clearly written, Soto Zen–based sharing of community-based practices that can help us heal from racism and other forms of structural violence, readers will benefit from this contemporary and unique Vietnamese American expression of socially engaged Buddhism that incorporates memoir, social justice analysis, and interactive practices."

—MUSHIM PATRICIA IKEDA, Buddhist teacher and author

"*Home Is Here* is an invaluable and engaging application of Buddhist teachings to racism, a topic important for all of us."

—GIL FRONSDAL, author of *Buddha Before Buddhism*

"This book will benefit everyone! Presenting a powerful and fresh look at core Buddhist teachings, it offers innovative and effective ways to free ourselves from the bondage and illusions of white supremacy culture and a compassionate, accessible path to experiencing that we are already whole."

—KAIRA JEWEL LINGO, author of *We Were Made for These Times*

"With tenderness, an open heart, and characteristic grace, Rev. Liên Shutt shares her knowledge and practice of Buddhadharma alongside her own searing experiences of being Asian American in our racialized culture. Far more than glib adaptations of the Buddha's Four Truths and Eightfold Path to contemporary life, Rev. Liên's thoughtful application of these central teachings of Buddhism to the process of undoing the harm of racism yields a body of innovative, meaningful, and heartfelt practices that invite the practitioner to encounter their lived experience with care and attention. Rev. Liên summarizes the place of each teaching in classical Buddhism, then explains carefully how her reframing applies in the context of healing and transforming the untold adverse impacts of white supremacist culture. Aware of the profundity of the inner work involved, Rev. Liên intersperses the substantive content with engaging practice instructions. The resulting pace marks a gentle but sure cadence to support the reader in their own discoveries. Anyone wishing to bring the wise compassion of the Buddha's teachings to bear on their journey with systemic oppression of any ilk will find in Rev. Liên a skillful and kind guide whose footsteps are well worth following."

—KARMA YESHE CHÖDRÖN, author of *Heal Transform Transcend*

"This book is an appropriate response—a clear, powerful, and kind Dharma that has emerged from the cauldron of a racialized and othered American society. In it, I hear Rev. Shutt's warmhearted care. This book is about tending to wounds with strong medicine, and it is about moving beyond healing, to build the strength to move forward in a new direction. That new direction is one which fulfills the promise of traditional Buddhism as a Path of liberation for all who make the effort to live it fully. The wisdom that she offers will surely open your eyes."

—AYYĀ DHAMMADĪPĀ, founder of Dassanāya Buddhist Community and author of *Gifts Greater than the Oceans*

"Reverend Liên Shutt's beautiful book is a treasure trove of Buddhist teachings shared from the heart and deep practice. You will not want to put it down once you open *Home Is Here*—filled with the voice of a kind Dharma companion guiding us on the path to healing and reconnecting with our whole self. Shutt's generosity, integrity and courage shines through on these pages."

—REBECCA LI, author of *Allow Joy into Our Hearts* and *Illumination*

"In *Home Is Here*, Rev. Liên Shutt extends the hand of spiritual friendship and invites us to walk the Eightfold Path in engaged companionship. By reciting her experiences as a queer Vietnamese American adoptee and Buddhist, she shows us that we can transform the pain of systemic othering by knowing suffering completely. More than a lofty Buddhist ideal, she provides the tools—from Engaged Eightfold factor framing and application to practice pauses—to skillfully delve into our suffering and emerge in wholeness, one breath at a time. In doing so, she offers *Home Is Here* as an invaluable resource to return to again and again: reminding us that home is where the engaged heart is."

—FUNIE HSU, associate professor of American studies, San Jose State University

"The Buddha was born to show us one important thing: that we are inherently perfectly whole in our Buddha nature. After enlightenment, the Buddha's very first teaching was the Four Noble Truths. After 2,500 years, this teaching remains a miracle remedy for the sufferings of sentient beings.

Through Rev. Liên's fresh view of the Engaged Four Noble Truths, everyone can find applicable ways to incorporate them into their own practice and eventually discover the true self where suffering doesn't exist."

—VEN. THÍCH NỮ THUẦN TUỆ, author of *Tâm Bình Thường* and *Từ Một Tâm Trong Lặng*

HOME
IS HERE

*Practicing Antiracism
with the
Engaged Eightfold Path*

Liên Shutt

North Atlantic Books
Huichin, unceded Ohlone land
Berkeley, California

Published by
North Atlantic Books   Cover art and design by Amit Malhotra
Huichin, unceded Ohlone land   Book design by Happenstance Type-O-Rama
Berkeley, California

Printed in the United States of America

Home Is Here: Practicing Antiracism with the Engaged Eightfold Path is sponsored and published by North Atlantic Books, an educational nonprofit based in the unceded Ohlone land Huichin (Berkeley, CA) that collaborates with partners to develop cross-cultural perspectives, nurture holistic views of art, science, the humanities, and healing, and seed personal and global transformation by publishing work on the relationship of body, spirit, and nature.

North Atlantic Books's publications are distributed to the US trade and internationally by Penguin Random House Publisher Services. For further information, visit our website at www.northatlantic books.com.

Library of Congress Cataloging-in-Publication Data

Names: Liên Shutt, T., author.
Title: Home is here : practicing antiracism with the engaged eightfold path
    / T. Liên Shutt.
Description: Berkeley : North Atlantic Books, 2023. | Includes
    bibliographical references. | Summary: "Builds on foundational Buddhist
    teachings, the Four Noble Truths and the Eightfold Path, offering an
    intersectional frame that helps you embody antiracist practices and tend
    to your own healing under racism and oppression"-- Provided by
    publisher.
Identifiers: LCCN 2022051773 (print) | LCCN 2022051774 (ebook) | ISBN
    9781623179045 (trade paperback) | ISBN 9781623179052 (ebook)
Subjects: LCSH: Race relations--Religious aspects--Buddhism. |
    Racism--Religious aspects--Buddhism.
Classification: LCC BQ4570.R3 L54 2023 (print) | LCC BQ4570.R3 (ebook) |
    DDC 294.3/376284--dc23/eng/20230206
LC record available at https://lccn.loc.gov/2022051773
LC ebook record available at https://lccn.loc.gov/2022051774

1 2 3 4 5 6 7 8 9 KPC 28 27 26 25 24 23

To Deb
Home is here—with you.

CONTENTS

PART I Seeing the World As-It-Is

PART II What the World Needs Now

PART III Realizing the Wholeness of the World

Our own life has to be our message.

—THICH NHAT HANH

FOREWORD

HERE IN NORTHERN CALIFORNIA, the past three years have been the driest on record. This parched season, I've been living on unceded Ohlone land. Not far south of me, you'll find the publisher of this capacious and liberatory book. Farther south and west, the Access to Zen (A2Z) meditation group is back to weekly in-person meetings. An hour's drive north of here is the Russian River, a place beloved by A2Z's guiding teacher Rev. Liên Shutt.

On early morning walks in my neighborhood, I pause to admire dew-dotted spiderwebs. Nestled among the leaves of succulents and shrubs, these tiny marvels yield their intricacies at daybreak, before the dew's departure paints them back into air. Like this book, each strand is made with tenderness and resilience.

I first encountered Rev. Liên in *Making the Invisible Visible—Healing Racism in Our Buddhist Communities,* a collection of writing by Buddhists of color and their allies. As a founding member of one of the few Bay Area POC meditation groups in the late 1990s, Shutt reflects:

> For many people of color and mixed-race people, because of our individual and collective histories of disenfranchisement, the need to find Refuge in a sangha is especially important. While each of us works toward the ability to be safe and free wherever we find ourselves in this present world, having a place that validates our essential being on a racial, ethnic, and cultural front is a necessary step in the process. It is my hope as a caretaker that the Buddhists of Color Sangha is such a place.

It is with this caretaking spirit and caretaker's resolve that Rev. Liên offers us *Home Is Here: Practicing Antiracism with the Engaged Eightfold Path*. In this long-awaited volume, we receive Dharma gifts in abundance: teachings to learn by, pauses to rest upon, stories to heal with, aspirations to live into.

As the opening lines of the introduction make clear, *Home Is Here* does not flinch from the many forms of violence that mar our world—violence that disproportionately harms those who have been marked as Other for reasons of race, gender, sexuality, class, and more. At the same time, this book refuses to reduce marginalized bodies to the harms visited upon them. As a Vietnamese American adoptee, 1.5-generation immigrant, and gender-nonconforming lesbian, Shutt is no stranger to suffering. With her decades of training as a Soto Zen priest and social worker, Rev. Liên also embodies the deep faith and defiant hope that inspire practitioners to proclaim the four bodhisattva vows:

> Beings are numberless, I vow to save them.
> Delusions are inexhaustible, I vow to end them.
> Dharma gates are boundless, I vow to enter them.
> Buddha's Way is unsurpassable, I vow to become it.

In *Home Is Here,* the snowy pappi of dandelions—weeds clinging to spiderwebs on the back porch of a home on the Russian River—become Dharma gates. This is a thirst-quenching book for those of us who yearn to weave Buddhist teachings with social justice, who wish to realize how the personal and the structural are in constant, cocreative relationship.

"I move from thinking my life is a cage to realizing it's a container," writes Rev. Liên. Reading *Home Is Here,* I feel as though I've been offered the begging bowl of the Soto Zen monk Ryokan (1758–1831):

> In my bowl
> I mingle
> Violets and dandelions,
> Wishing to offer them
> To the buddhas in the three worlds
> *(trans. Kazuaki Tanahashi)*

With a kindred spirit of urgency and sincerity, Ryokan's contemporary, the Japanese poet and lay Buddhist priest Kobayashi Issa (1763–1828), composed the following haiku after the death of his young daughter:

> This dewdrop world—
> Is a dewdrop world,
> And yet, and yet . . .
>> *(trans. Lewis Mackenzie)*

Begging bowl, spiderweb, dandelion pappus, dewdrop, Rev. Liên, you, me: each a humble container vast enough to encompass the entire cosmos.

May this book aid us in finding home right where we are, even as we strive to create Refuge for all.

Chenxing Han
November 2022

PREFACE

THIS BOOK DID NOT start out as a book. This book came into being as a response.

In the spring of 2020, as the world was shutting down due to COVID-19, cries for help and support arose from my students. The largest in number and in degree were from students of Asian ancestry. Some of those cries were about the pandemic, but the majority were about how to deal with the fear, distress, anger, despair, and a variety of other emotions due to the stark increase of Asian American animus and violence. As the devastating consequences of COVID-19 started to become obvious with the steep rise in deaths, the cause for it was still unclear and blame started to be thrown around. In the United States, this became yet another example of the kind of hatred targeted to its people of Asian ancestry as we heard "Chinese virus" and "Kung Flu" from the highest office in our country, emboldening others to violence both online and on the streets.

As a Buddhist teacher, my work is to respond to suffering. When the suffering was being experienced by my Asian American students in the San Francisco Bay area, I realized that a curriculum I was developing called the Engaged Four Noble Truths was the answer. Since the fall of 2017, I was in the midst of reformatting the most ancient and basic of Buddhist teachings, the Four Noble Truths, which are often taught simply as a way to understand how suffering and its causes can be overcome individually. I was reframing them to include how structural and systemic causes need to be emphasized so that these teachings can be more relevant to our current times generally, and to social justice more specifically. As I see them, they are applicable to all locations and apply to all realms of personal development or distress, systemic crises, disenfranchisement, and oppressions. In particular, they can and have been used these past few years to address and respond to the COVID-19 pandemic, to genderphobia, to homophobia, and to racialization and racism.

My work on this reframing actually started in response to another set of distressing events. Beginning in early 2017, the North American Buddhist world was rocked by several incidences of sexual misconduct by well-known teachers. This issue was a focus at a gathering of my contemporary teachers, and a social work model of conflict resolution and restoration was presented. Being a social worker myself, I found that model to be very useful, but I left the gathering wondering what Buddhist teachings could be used in addition. Other issues, including communication conflicts, gender disparity, racism, and homophobia, had been making other waves in practice communities for some time, and it had been my experience that the reconciliation training models brought in to address these issues came from *outside* of Buddhist teachings.

After much reflection, studies, and discussions with teachers and peers, I started formulating what I call the Engaged Four Noble Truths. This work was met with support by the Hemera Foundation. My exploration of these Truths is based on whether they can serve as a restorative framework for any critical need. In particular, I was interested in their potential when applied to oppressive forces and systems such as any of the isms.

In the fall of 2019, I started to teach these Engaged Four Noble Truths in a broad way as part of an eight-month studies program with my students of Access to Zen, my home *sangha,* a community of practitioners. Then, in 2020, as a response to the general call for support around the pandemic, as a nine-week course. However, given the expansive race-wall of North American society, echoed in convert Buddhist settings, race has always been the edge of my practice. Thus, when the calls for help and support came from Asian American practitioners from various sanghas in the San Francisco Bay Area, it seemed timely and crucial to put these Engaged Four Noble Truths to the test. This is how the four-month course, A Lotus Rising from Mud: A Path for Asian American Restoration, came into being.

As Lotus was in preparation, the murder of George Floyd was caught on camera, and the resulting new round of demands for racial justice grew nationally and worldwide. I was already in conversation with the teachers of a Sonoma-area temple about their desire to build a more racially diverse sangha (mine is one of the very few in the area). We decided to offer a class to meet that critical call. Thus, The Dharma of Being Antiracist: Accessing the Eightfold Path for Skillful Engagement (DBA) was also born. Its structure was the same as Lotus except that it was a team of racially diverse teachers of various configurations of races (depending on the iteration), though we were very firm in our 50-50 makeup of BIPOCs (Black, Indigenous, and people of color) and white participants.

Both Lotus and the Dharma of Being Antiracist (DBA) are built on the premise that the Engaged Four Noble Truths and its Engaged Eightfold Path can serve as a restorative container that meets the needs of our complex modern world. It does this because it's both descriptive and prescriptive in individual and structural ways, showing us how we can know and enact liberation for ourselves and for all beings.

There is hurt and harm in our world. So much of it is powered by greed, hatred, and the delusion of separateness. It has been so rewarding to have been with so many practitioners and to see how these teachings, when engaged mindfully, wholeheartedly, and with sincerity, have brought healing and restoration for so many.

This book is a response, offering a possibility of healing and restoring racial harm through a reframing of the classic Four Noble Truths, the most fundamental of Buddhist teachings, as a means to return to our individual and collective wholeness.

You are invited to join us on this Path to wholeness. May it be of benefit to you and all beings.

CONTENT WARNING

PLEASE READ WITH CARE as this book shares stories of the experiences and impacts of systems of oppression generally, and of racism in particular.

While I will be offering the practices of Buddhism and the Engaged Four Noble Truths and its Engaged Eightfold Path in these pages as ways that have supported me to transform the traumas of racism and other oppressions, it is work built upon many years of practice, therapy, and social justice work, supported by many teachers and professionals. By no means will the teachings and practices in this book format, broadly or via the Practice Pauses, be a substitute or replacement for professional help. Please seek such support when needed.

INTRODUCTION

THE WHOLENESS OF LIFE
Location. Location. Location.

"Where are you from? . . . No, no, *really,* where are you from?"

"Hey, Chink! Go home!"

"People like you shouldn't live in this neighborhood."

"I was in your country and saved your people."

"Why do you act like a white girl?"

"You're a Twinkie,* aren't you?"

"Buddhism came to America some forty-nine or fifty years ago."

"Don't you know this is the women's restroom?"

"F***king lesbian!"

○ ○ ○ ○

In each moment we are located.
In lineage. In ancestry.
By others. By ourselves.
By sight. By perception. By differentiation. By discrimination.
By institutions. By policies. By governmental structures. By systems of
   oppressions.

---

* *Twinkie:* derogatory term for an Asian North American as being "yellow on the outside, white on the inside."

By homophobia. By sexism. By genderphobia.
By white supremacy culture. By racism.
By erasure. By invisibilization. By exclusion.
   By inclusion. By equity. By love.
With hatred. With fear. With anxiety.
   With love. With care. With tenderness. With joy.
In isolation.
   In community. In belonging. In the world.
In time. In space.
In Emptiness.
In wholeness.

○ ○ ○ ○

As a Vietnamese American adoptee, 1.5-generation,* immigrant, cisgender female, gender-nonconforming, lesbian, Soto Zen priest, and in the late mid-years of a chronological life, I am often located by others, as I don't always present or behave in ways people believe my social locations to be. For instance, I'm often asked as I'm entering a washroom, "Don't you know this is the women's restroom?" Perhaps, it could be because of my shaved head due to being a priest, but, likely, it's also because I have been nonconforming in the ways I've carried myself for most of my life, in gender and other socially prescribed manners.

When I was in Vietnam in 2002 and traveling with Vietnamese and Vietnamese American friends, they would often ask me to stay in the van as they went in to negotiate the lodging price. This was due to the unofficial but commonly used tiered pricing scale: lowest for current Vietnamese nationals, next level for Vietnamese in diaspora, and most expensive for foreigners. According to my friends, while my ethnic identity was visually apparent, the way I held myself was "American." They felt that I exuded "too much confidence" and took up "too much space" compared to a typical Vietnamese female.

---

* *1.5 generation* refers to someone who immigrated as a child or teenager and thus has a different experience than either a first- or second-generation immigrant.

For most of my life, I have had to be hyperaware of my social locations wherever I am, especially of locations imputed on me by systems of oppression. By location, I mean a framing for how an individual is designated a position in specific systems, and, with it, the assumptions and privileges (or lack of them) that come with it. This framing of locationality allows for an understanding that an identity always comes with embedded social power that can change depending on which system is operating in each moment of interaction with another, interpersonally and in structures. For instance, as an able-bodied Vietnamese American, I am located in a down-power* position or location (less privilege) within the system of white supremacy, yet I am in an up-power (more privilege) location in ableism. Understanding one's location is important because, depending on the embedded lack of or privilege of power, one's responsibility changes.

I have tried to grasp solidly onto some of these locations at times, trying hard to be "American" or "Vietnamese" for others and for myself. At other times I've tried rejecting locations, especially those imputed on me by others and by systems. I've done both in many ways: individually and with others; through academic studies, art, therapy, volunteerism, activism, and work as a social worker.

Then finally, when my suffering couldn't be processed thoroughly through those means, I leaned into my Buddhist practice. At first, it was out of utter confusion. After my graduate studies, I went back to Vietnam for the first time after twenty-eight years. I thought I was "going home," but after five months I realized that the "home" I envisioned was simply that: a vision, carried from my past and my childhood. This threw me for a loop, and I came back to the United States utterly shaken.

Who am I? Where do I belong?

I had been practicing lay Buddhism for almost six years by then. With this shattering of old ideas about myself, I then decided to go to a monastery in Northern California to do some intensive meditation, chanting,

---

* Down- and up-power positioning is from Cedar Barstow's work in *Right Use of Power: The Heart of Ethics,* 10th Anniversary Edition (Boulder, CO: Many Realms Publishing, 2015).

and other Buddhist practices. Initially, my aim was a three-month intensive retreat, but I ended up staying for three and a half years and ordaining as a priest in the Soto Zen tradition.

Fast-forward to more than two decades later and, with the years of practice and being a Buddhist and meditation teacher, I have developed a more complete sense of how to hold my experiences of social locations in ways that are more grounding yet responsive, fostering healing and restoration.

In the Soto Zen tradition, when I'm asked to give a Dharma talk, it is customary at the beginning for me to thank the abbatial leader of the temple and the Tanto, who is the head of practice and the person whose job it is to invite me. Next, I thank my teachers. All this is part of locating. It's not just common courtesy; it's to locate me in a lineage and a sect of Buddhism, and in a lineage of practitioners.

Locating ourselves has significance; it takes effort and intentional attention to honor where we come from and who we are.

At another place where I teach, we invite people to say what land they are on currently to honor the Indigenous peoples and also as an act of anti-oppression by acknowledging we're on stolen land. We also invite people to share their pronouns as a way to say that we're inclusive of gender diversity. Other social locations that are often shared, depending on which community of practitioners I'm teaching or practicing with, are sexual orientation, class, ability, immigration status, and neurodiversity.

These are all frames of reference for knowing where and how we inhabit our locations, specifically in different systems of oppression.

It can also locate us in communities and, therefore, in systems of joy and of belonging. At the same time, part of our practice is about having a sense that there is fluidity and that these ways of self-identification or of being perceived by others are not all we are. As practitioners of Buddhism, we want to be aware that identity arises due to present causes and conditions.

Therefore, how we all come to be here in this place, at this moment, is always in context.

ZEN INSIGHT

Speaking of context, as you go into this book, you may ask yourself: Is this Zen* or Insight† Buddhism? The answer is, it's both! While born as a Pure Land Buddhist in Vietnam, I started my meditation training in the North American Insight Tradition and then "stumbled" into North American Soto Zen. While I love what I call the "cheerleader" aspect of Soto Zen because it posits that we are all enlightened already but just don't know it due to our unskillful conditioning, its basic practice is simply to be with life as-it-is and, therefore, often does not provide a lot of explanation. So, while the gist of this book is to remind us of our inherent wholeness, I also acknowledge that it takes active intention and engagement *to be confident in this knowing and to act from such aspiration.* Hence, I combine the two styles of practice in my teaching as they offer a middle way between not enough information for clarity of understanding and too conceptual with an overemphasis on how-tos. I hope I have achieved a balance within these pages.

It is said that the Buddha taught that the teachings should be appropriate to the audience, time, and place. As such, while I want to be very clear that the content of this book comes from my understanding and practice of Buddhism, the aim of these teachings is that they are for everyone.

FIND YOURSELF HERE

This book is for all who have been hurt and harmed by the system of white supremacy and other systemic wrongs, and for those seeking restoration and healing. As shared, I started this book to be an accompanying text for my courses on how to work with the impacts of racism. Both the Lotus

---

* While I acknowledge there are many Buddhist practice traditions that have been translated into English as "Zen," when used by itself in this book, I'm referring to the Japanese Zen sect I've most practiced: Soto Zen.

† "Insight" is an English translation for Vipassana. However, as *Vipassana* means both the Theravada sect of Buddhism and a whole class of meditation methods, I will use "Insight" when talking about the sect.

Rising from Mud and the Dharma of Being Antiracist courses are based on working with formative memories of being conditioned, and at times coerced, to "inhabit" another's imputations of our racialized location. Many participants in these courses wanted a text that was more contemporary and germane than much of what is currently available, that expanded on the topics that came up in the Q&A and discussions, and that would offer more than what could be covered in the format of a class.

As I taught these courses and started to think about a book, memories of practice incidents that involved racism or other oppressive forces arose that illuminated each of the Eightfold Path factors. In all honesty, I resisted having this book be so memoir-ish for a long time. However, I realized that if I was asking people who took the courses to be open and vulnerable, and to keep engaging with their challenging memories of racialization and racism, then I, too, had to do the same.

Additionally, writing this book has helped me to clarify the distinction between when self-work is needed and when structural work is needed. As I see it, when we're in the down-power position in a system of oppression, it is essential to work on our individual healing from the hatred we've experienced and to heal the hurt and harm we've internalized from such a location. If we're in the up-power position in a system of oppression, then our function is to work to heal the *structure* of that oppression. Maintaining wholeness is both individual work and structural, in-community work. Thus, in terms of racism, as an Asian American, self-healing is necessary and ongoing work for me to access and maintain well-being. However, as a person with a graduate degree and therefore labor access, I need to be mindful of, and help activate, class equity in an organization, policy, or other structural formulations as a function of being anti-classist. My hope is that this book will help you discern for yourself which kind of work is needed when.

Lastly, if you're yearning for a sense of wholeness for the state of our world, then this book will be a benefit to you. Perhaps, like myself, you are an activist or social justice worker who keeps finding yourself at the point of compassion fatigue and burnout. Again, while I have focused on race, these teachings work for other forms of oppressions and challenges because, fundamentally, these Engaged Four Noble Truths are based on understanding how we were taught to frame, believe in, and act out old beliefs. This book is about how to meet with groundedness and clarity our conditioning from systems of domination. Additionally, to learn, through the practices of the Engaged Eightfold Path in these pages, that we have a choice to not participate in and perpetuate these systems anymore. To be able to throw off such old trappings in body, heart, and mind is a liberation that is available to all and applicable in all realms of life.

The teachings and practices to live from wholeness within ourselves and with each other is the offering of the Dharma. These teachings are available to everyone, always. May these Engaged Four Noble Truths and Engaged Eightfold Path—a contemporary, restorative-focused reframing of these ancient teachings—be of service to you.

MY OFFERING TO YOU

For me, the system of white supremacy culture and racism, as one of its results, has been the oppressive force that has been most painful, harming, and enduring. It classifies, stratifies, and enforces constructed racial categories. I have worked hard to learn about it and extricate myself from it through studies, activism, and work to address its impact. All these experiences of learning have been useful. However, Buddhism brought a framing to these issues in a way that has been freeing. After practicing and teaching Buddhism for over twenty-five years, I have come to realize how any single social location that I have been taught, internalized, experienced, and imputed on by others *is not one that is solid nor enduring.* There is a way to understand, be with, and then find empowerment and the agency to use our locations when useful or skillful and yet *not be used by them.* There are ways to reframe our understanding and experiences by freeing ourselves from constructs.

This book is an exploration of how this can be achieved through the Engaged Four Noble Truths as applied to race and racialization. It also describes and provides a means for healing and restoration from the impacts of white supremacy culture's racism in ways that support your reframing of them in experiential ways.

As such, the book is laid out in three parts, which echoes the traditional layout of the Eightfold Path and yet is modified to reflect a restorative model. For instance, the Eightfold Path, while having eight factors, is traditionally broken into three groupings, presented in this progression:

Wisdom: Includes the factors of Skillful View and Skillful Thinking

Ethical Conduct: Includes the factors of Skillful Speech, Skillful Action, and Skillful Livelihood

Meditative: Includes the factors of Skillful Effort, Skillful Mindfulness, and Skillful Concentration

In this book, as has been found to be efficacious in the various Lotus Rising from Mud and the Dharma of Being Antiracist courses, I've dispersed the meditative factors of Skillful Effort, Skillful Mindfulness, and Skillful Concentration within the other two groupings to support readers and practitioners as we go through the challenges of working through our racial conditioning within white supremacy culture and its racism. Additionally, as part of what I find to be essential to a restorative model, the book is laid out into what I would term as three essential aspects of healing from trauma:

- Acknowledging what is,
- Knowing what shifts are especially needed, and
- Learning how to put those shifts into practice.

The book is then divided into these three parts with the corresponding Eightfold Path factors (with reframed names that are explained in their corresponding chapters):

Part I: Seeing the World As-It-Is:

- **Skillful View** is presented in two chapters. First, to fully present the Engaged Four Noble Truths. Second, we'll look at karma, racial conditioning, and social locations in systems of domination.

- **Skillful Concentration** is the meditative quality that supports us to be with the challenges of acknowledging the deep hurt and harm of white supremacy culture.

Part II: What the World Needs Now:

- **Skillful Motivation** describes how we can change our conditioned beliefs to reflect our own contemporary values, which inclines us toward social justice and restoration.

- **Skillful Effort** gives us clear guidance for ways to transform unwholesome karmic seeds and to cultivate new wholesome ones.

- **Skillful Mindfulness** will give us the wherewithal to move from surviving to thriving.

- **Skillful Speech** shifts the focus of communication, transforming internalized racism or privileges embedded in our location in white supremacy culture.

Part III: Realizing the Wholeness of the World:

- **Skillful Enacting** from wholeness is seeing how the precepts can guide us to actualize our nonharming commitments.

- **Skillful Living** offers ways to work with life energies we've discovered on the Path to sustain wholeness in our lives.

Each chapter of the book is laid out in three sections to emphasize how these practices can be applied in our everyday life in the world. First, I offer a personal memory that illuminated for me that Eightfold factor, followed by the teachings on that aspect. Lastly, I share how these teachings support restoration by giving examples of how that Eightfold factor clarifies and supports us to be with, work with, or respond to racialization and the impacts of white supremacy culture.

Practice Pauses

Realizing that the willingness to read a book on the hurt and harm of racism takes courage and commitment, I would like to offer a few ways to engage with it. First, know that this is a practice book. By this, I mean that, while I've taken the time to give it a format that seeks to provide a restorative flow, which came from it being "tested" in my two courses, this is not a textbook or workbook. While "information" is within these pages as a necessity to sharing the Eightfold Path teachings and their practices, this book is really an offering for a healing journey of your own. As such, I recommend that you read this book slowly, pausing to let whatever is coming up for you within these pages to resonate. To support this, I've offered "Practice Pauses" at various places within each chapter. These are meditations, reflection writings, or mindfulness practices that a reader can try as ways to either experientially enact the practice I'm sharing, or simply as an intentional check-in with yourself and the feelings, sensations, or thoughts that are coming up.

Additionally, these practices are indexed in the appendix so that you can return to engage with them as a support to you at any time. Please do take your time with these Practice Pauses and never "push through" if they are activating in any way. Our overall aim of these restorative practices is to trust in our innate wisdom and bring caring mindfulness to all we do.

Remember that work to transform our suffering takes time and, while individual effort is needed, also calls for other supportive means and people. As such, the teachings and practices in this book format, broadly or via the Practice Pauses, are not a substitute nor a replacement for the courses mentioned in this book nor other forms of professional help. Please seek such support when needed.

THE NET OF INDRA

In the Avatamsaka Sutra, the Net of Indra is depicted as a system of strands crisscrossing each other to form a net. At the nodes, where the strands connect, there are sparkling jewels. Because of the reflective nature of jewels, each mirrors the others. It is said that this is a metaphor for how we are interconnected.

This description of the Net of Indra is a beautiful teaching about interconnectedness. However, I would like to bring in another way to view it. Rather than focusing so much on the jewels, our focus can be more on the net itself. Imagine that we're all jewels in this big net. Due to privilege, the jewel with the most resources swells up bigger and bigger, becoming heavier and heavier, stretching the strands of the net that holds us all together. Then, when the heavy, swollen jewel causes enough strain, there might be a tear in the net, causing other jewels to fall. Or, perhaps, as the jewel swells up bigger and bigger, it takes over more and more space, pushing out the other jewels or covering up their ability to shine.

When we focus only on the jewels—when we think the jewels are more important than the *integrity* of the net—then the wholeness of the net suffers.

Often, when discussions on race, race relations, or racial justice occur in predominantly white convert Buddhist circles, people of color are often told to "let go of your sense of separation" and get on the bandwagon of "oneness" that's supposed to be what Buddhist teachings are about. I want to propose this instead: our practice isn't that we should all be the *same-size jewels*; rather, our practice is to see and be stewards of *the whole net*.

To see and attend to the whole net, we can ask ourselves, how are the strands made up? What are the conditions that lead to some jewels being overly heavy by taking up too many resources? Where have we allowed the net to fray or be torn, causing gaps? How have we been historically conditioned to not take care of that part of the net and thus not nourish the jewels in that section of our world?

The net is the wholeness that we're trying to maintain or create.

Back in 2015, I was invited to give a Dharma talk on the fiftieth anniversary of the Selma to Montgomery March to protest the blocking of voting rights of African Americans by segregation laws in Alabama. Preparing for the talk, the Net of Indra came up as a means to remind us of our interconnection. Additionally, having studied the Matrix of Oppression,[1] I knew of the sociological paradigm of the interrelatedness of systems of oppression: How one's degree of power, or privileges, change dependent on one's social location within the context of race, class, and gender.

For instance, a person of color always has less privilege when interacting with a white-identified person in the system of racism, but if the person of color has more economic access than the white person, then the power dynamics are more complex. Also, when a person lives being oppressed by more than one system of domination, the interrelatedness of these systems further adds to their oppression. Thus, the strength of any strands on the net between the jewels are dependent on many conditions. This paradigm became clear to me at that time, as a better way to elucidate the "oneness" of Buddhist teachings as focusing more on the net than the jewels. As such, I'll be using the Net of Indra as a metaphor for the wholeness of life as inclusive of our lives as individuals *and* the connections between us.

Essentially, this book is an offering for how to attend to ourselves from the hurts and harms of white supremacy culture or other oppressions. As you'll see early on, pausing and assessing is part of what makes these practices of the Engaged Four Noble Truths capable of providing us with the framing and skillful means to restore and heal.

They have done so for me and the many participants of the related courses. May they do so for you also.

Thank you for your bravery and courage to transform yourself and the world we all share together.

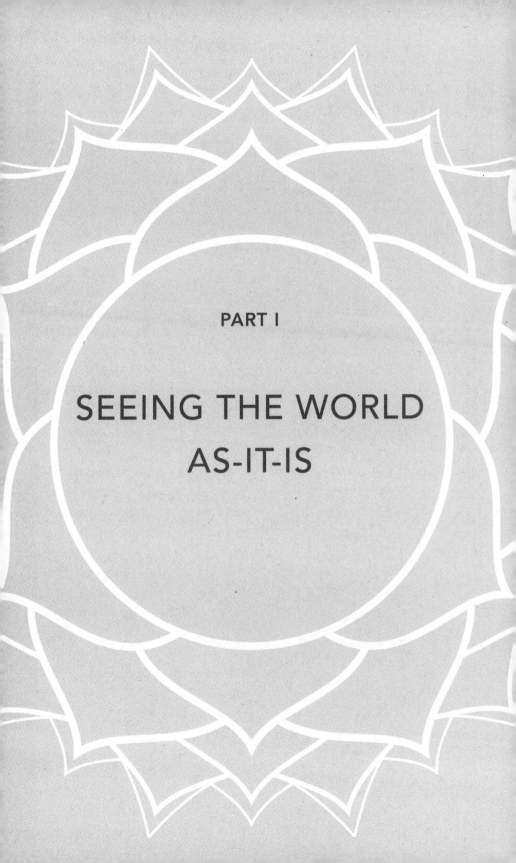

PART I

SEEING THE WORLD AS-IT-IS

THE ENGAGED FOUR NOBLE TRUTHS
We Are Complete and Whole

THE RING OF A BELL signaled it was my turn for *dokusan,* an interview to discuss my practice with the Soto Zen Master at this five-hundred-year-old training monastery in Japan.

I picked up a small mallet and struck the cast iron bell in front of me: one time, letting it ring, then a second time. I rose and hurried down a long hall of tatami mats, the woven straw flooring in traditional Japanese living spaces, passing through the Ihai-do, a narrow room lined on both sides with rows of individual altars for deceased sangha community members. They silently witnessed the swish of cloth as my long black priest robe rubbed back and forth around my ankles with each quick step.

At the end of the hall, three steps rose up. I stopped at the bottom and performed a short *gassho,* bowing with palms touching and elbows out. Then in one swift motion, I grabbed the end of my *zagu,* or priest bowing cloth, laid it down on the tatami, and folded it into a square. I dropped down and started my full prostrations as quickly as possible— body crouched in child's pose, both hands outstretched and palms placed up on the floor, then, with symmetrical precision, hands raised past the ears and down again before rising to stand. I did this three times quickly, as is the custom, after which I refolded and slid the zagu back over my left wrist. One more quick gassho and then I headed up those three stairs to my dokusan with Sekkei Harada Roshi, the Abbot of Hosshinji monastery in Obama, Japan. I entered the room ready to ask *the* central question of my life.

I had come to Japan after leaving the predominantly white convert Soto Zen Buddhist monastery in Central California where I had thought I would spend the rest of my life. When I had asked to be ordained after more than eight years of meditative Buddhist practice, I had felt a deep calling to live as a Buddhist monastic. But this did not come to be. I left the California monastery after three and a half years there, heartbroken and confused about the racism I had experienced on both a personal and structural level. The persistent white supremacy culture of the monastery made it unsafe and did not support me as a Vietnamese American practitioner. This was true for many other people of color staying there as well. The experience was a huge shock to my understanding of Buddhism, Buddhist practice, and my sense of place in the world.

As I made plans to leave that California monastery and figure out how to practice as a newly ordained priest, I was contacted by someone who studied under Sekkei Harada Roshi in Japan. They urged me to study with him as he was acknowledged as an enlightened Zen Master. I had only practiced Soto Zen in predominantly white convert settings in the United States and I felt drawn to practice in Japan, the birthplace of this sect of Buddhism.

I had been at Hosshinji for three weeks, trying to process my despair from having to leave California due to the racism at my home monastery. There was another American at the monastery, a white woman. Instead of being someone I could connect with, she had harassed me, saying things like, "You're good for nothing! You're trash!" in hissed whispers as we moved about the various ceremonies and tasks of the temple. I couldn't get away from her either—we were housed in the same nuns' quarters together, we had come to Hosshinji around the same time so we had similar seniority, and we were the same height so we were often paired together for ceremonies.

Her hateful whispers seemed to follow me all over the temple. The racism I had experienced in California had followed me all the way to Japan.

Entering the room for dokusan with Sekkei Harada Roshi, I barely sat down before blurting out the quintessential question of my existence up to that moment. "Why does hatred seem to follow me wherever I go?" I asked.

Sekkei Harada didn't hesitate. "Know hatred completely," he answered. Then he grabbed the handbell to his right and rang it vigorously, signaling the end to my interview.

I scrambled out of the room, doing the prostrations and bows in reverse order.

My mind raced to make meaning of what had just happened.

Nothing came.

My mind had stopped.

○ ○ ○ ○

A koan in Zen practice is a story assigned by a teacher for you to work with. Various traditions have different ways of practicing with koans, but giving an answer to the teacher as part of the process is a commonality across sects. How the teacher accepts or rejects the answer is part of the mythology of this practice. A well-known koan is, "At this very moment, what is your original face before your parents were born?"

Many people think koans are paradoxes, but really they're stories to stop your mind, to bump it off its loop of incessant and well-worn patterns of thinking, planning, and processing. Koans open us to an understanding that's beyond habitual thinking.

Life also gives us koans.

For me, racism has been a koan I've turned over and over. Studying race theory was one of my answers to this koan. Other answers from my life have included activism and various jobs as a social worker focused on addressing the harmful results of racism.

All of these were good answers.

In Zen, we like to say, "The question is more important than the answer." Why? Because questions often come up at uncomfortable moments. Deep questions arise when we're faced with circumstances in which our coping mechanisms aren't working anymore. At such moments, transformational change is possible if we stay open to all answers, especially unexpected ones.

The system of white supremacy centers whiteness, and makes itself subject, while juxtaposing people of color as "other," fragmenting us all into the delusion of separateness. Aware of this dynamic and its harm to people of color, I had to be careful to not simply search outside myself for answers. Like many Asian Americans and other people of color, at some point I had to learn to value myself, reclaiming the validity of my own experience in any moment and in any condition. Buddhist practice over many years has supported me to return to knowing and trusting my wholeness.

"Know hatred completely." That moment with Roshi stopped my mind from its habitual looping to try to "understand" racism. All my intellectual theories and years of antiracist work didn't address my suffering in a useful way at this crucial point of my life. That moment stopped my frantic search to find some reason why hatred kept following me. What I needed was to *attend* to the hurt and harm from being the *target* of racism.

In Buddhism, we practice to be able to find settledness and clarity that's not dependent on the conditions of the world. To find such settledness and clarity, we have to attend to our suffering in body, heart, and mind. The koan of racism was not just something that I wanted to understand. What I really want, even now, is to heal from the hurt and pain I've carried.

In both activist and Buddhist practice realms, I felt that I had to choose between a rock and a hard place. For example, in feminist spaces, white women were most often touted as leaders, negating the many ways women of color brought groundbreaking exploration and transformation to gender oppression. Or in racial justice groups, male-identified BIPOCs often take up the most space, including leadership ones. Or, in many of the convert-based meditation groups I've taught at, I am thought to be "too religious," especially as Buddhism-based practices have been appropriated into secularized popular "mindfulness" apps and health and self-care industries.

Similarly, I noticed that in predominantly white convert Buddhist centers, people of color were often told that race was not part of practice because "there's no self." When I tried to address racist incidents, I was told that this was to reify "a false sense of self." If antiracism work was acknowledged by white leaders, then it was "just a relative stepping stone" on the way to an "absolute." By default, given the predominantly white and mostly male teachers within convert Buddhism in North America, this "absolute" felt patriarchal, white-defined, and white-centered.

I needed a way to practice that started from the premise that there is racism in the world and that there are intense manifestations of it in the United States of America. Racism impacts us on the cushion, in meditation halls, in practice communities, in our places of work, in conversations with friends, at the doctor's office, and everywhere we go. This is true whether we are people of color or white identified. I needed a way to practice Buddhism that moved from only an individual focus to one that recognized the power and privilege embedded in our structures and systems and how we are impacted by them in different ways. In doing so, I hoped to discover how to heal from systemic hurts and harms also.

THE ENGAGED FOUR NOBLE TRUTHS

What does it mean to attend to our suffering in body, heart, and mind when racism can cause such intense hurt and harm? We need a way to orient our sense of the world. In Buddhism, the teachings start with the Four Noble Truths. People have been practicing with them deeply and widely for almost 2,600 years. Classically, they are listed in this way:

> In life, there is suffering.
>
> There are roots for the arising of suffering.
>
> There is an end to suffering.
>
> The Eightfold Path is the way to end suffering.

In an effort to practice with these Four Noble Truths in a way that reso-
nated with my lived experience of racism in the system of white supremacy, I've developed a version that focuses on how they can be used to
actively address the suffering and injustices in our contemporary lives.
While applied primarily to race in this work, this framing can be used as
healing and restoration from other systemic injustices as well. I call these
the Engaged Four Noble Truths:

> Harm and harming are present.
>
> Understand fully the causes and conditions for harm and harming.
>
> Individual and collective agency for ending harm is possible.
>
> The Eightfold Path empowers wholeness.

Additionally, each of the Four Noble Truths have a practice instruction
associated with them: investigate, abandon, realize, and develop. These
instructions offer us ways to understand and practice each of these Truths
as applied to my Engaged version:

> **Investigate** what harm and harming is present.
>
> Once we understand fully the causes and conditions for harm and
> harming, we **abandon** such unskillful thoughts and behaviors.
>
> In doing so, we **realize** individual and collective agency for ending
> harm is possible.
>
> The **Eightfold Path** empowers wholeness and thus **needs to be
> developed.**

As we can see, there is a real elegance to how these practice instructions
have been laid out for us. This, essentially, is the clear purpose of the Buddhist Four Noble Truths: to provide us a clear means to be with, work
with, gain confidence in their ending, and then develop skillful means to
be with *dukkha,* or suffering. Let's see how they, reframed as the Engaged
Four Noble Truths, further offer us a way to apply these teachings and
their instructions as applied to anti-oppression in general, and antiracism
in particular.

Engaged First Noble Truth
Harm and Harming Are Present

The First Noble Truth is the hardest to be with. Mostly we spend our energy trying to ignore harm and harming in our lives, and if that's not possible, we try to get away from it or deny its existence. This is true in race-based incidents as well. Racial incidents are often ignored, avoided, or denied, creating more harm and harming.

However, if we can meet our experience fully, we can learn to live in the truth that harm and harming are present and not become overwhelmed by it. For example, with the First Noble Truth, the practice instruction is to "investigate" dukkha. We're asked to identify and be aware of the full range of dukkha, the Pali* word that's often translated as suffering, dis-ease, dissatisfaction, and discontent—or harm and harming in the Engaged version. To be able to find answers to dukkha, we have to fully investigate, or explore more and more, how it shows up in our lives. Investigating harm and harming shows us where wholeness has been broken, disrupted, or torn. In the teachings, dukkha is described with the metaphor of an axle that doesn't fit well into the hub of a wheel, preventing the wheel from turning smoothly. Our practice, then, is to investigate to see how we can find ways to know how to make the wheel turn smoothly again.

That's the First Noble Truth. The Second shows us the causes and conditions that have resulted in the imbalance of the axle and wheel. The Third reminds us that it's possible for the cart to roll smoothly again. The Fourth Noble Truth—the Eightfold Path—will give us very specific ways to know, develop, and put into practice the skillful means so that axle, wheel, and cart work together harmoniously again.

---

* In general, Pali is considered the first known recorded language of Buddhism and is the language of Theravada Buddhist texts. Sanskrit is the language of Mahayana Buddhist texts, which includes Zen.

However, just like remembering the net instead of just focusing on the jewels in the Net of Indra, I want to remind us that when we are noticing dukkha, it is also a moment that we "wake up" to how, in seeing the disruption, we're also identifying it in the midst of wholeness. In the moment when we've identified hurt and harm, we're also calling attention to how wholeness needs to be repaired. So when we notice suffering, we can ask, how can I come back to the equilibrium and clarity of wholeness? When we're working to rectify harm and harming, we are actually seeking ways to return to wholeness. To me, while diligent effort is definitely needed for healing and restoration, we need to remember that when we're working to address oppressions, it's a reclaiming of our inherent wholeness. And thus, it's not about what is lacking in us; more about returning to ourselves, inhabiting the home that is always here, individually and collectively.

This is a key way to reframe how those of us who call out and then work to rectify injustices are actually champions of wholeness. For instance, when racism is named in a situation, it could be a signal that equality is not present, equity is not present, justice is not present, or love and compassion are not present. To recognize that wholeness is missing is to seek restoration. Instead of starting from dukkha as something lacking or wrong, we can start from our knowledge of wholeness as already present and possible. This means that as a Vietnamese American woman, I know that there's nothing wrong with me if someone questions where I'm really from for the hundredth time. My sense of wholeness is present and possible. This is a supportive and uplifting way to frame our practice with these Truths.

There's a story about when the Buddha was young that points us to a sense of wholeness. Before he was enlightened, the Buddha was called Gautama. One day, Gautama accompanied his father, the king, to one of the farms of their kingdom for the spring planting festivities. Toward the afternoon, Gautama found himself alone, sitting under a rose apple tree, as his attendants had gone off to join the plowing. There, seated in the shade on a hot day, Gautama realized that he had a sense of wholeness, and that everything was well. In some teachings it is said that this is one of the things the Buddha remembered years later as he sat under the Bodhi tree trying to attain his enlightenment.

PRACTICE PAUSE
Connecting to Wholeness Meditation

You can try this, too. Take a moment to connect to a sense of wholeness as if you were sitting* under that rose apple tree, or perhaps a tree from your childhood, or by a lake or the ocean, or somewhere in nature that brings you a sense of peace and wholeness.

Rest and relax into this place.

Let yourself fully *be* in this moment of stillness and rest, where there's nothing for you to do. Just rest as-you-are in this moment as-it-is: whole and complete.

As you focus on the feeling of wholeness, I invite you to connect it to a spot within your actual physical body, somewhere that's very visceral: perhaps in the weight of your body at the sitting bones of your posture or the fullness of your belly at the end of an inhale. Let yourself rest there and know it fully.

This is a place that you can return to at any point in time, to know an innate sense of wholeness.

---

* Sitting, standing, walking, or lying down are all positions the Buddha recommended, so feel free to take a meditative position that works for you. I am writing "sitting" here only to stay with the story of Gautama sitting under the tree.

Engaged Second Noble Truth
Understand Fully the Causes and Conditions for Harm and Harming

The Engaged Second Noble Truth is similar to its traditional counterpart by pointing us toward examining the roots that lead to the arising of suffering. The Engaged version directs more specifically the need to look at the ways we've been conditioned and how this conditioning came to us, individually and systemically. We can ask ourselves, how were we taught to be with experiences of harm or harming? Did they come from our families or our cultures? How did systemic structures such as racism, ableism, transphobia, heterosexism, homophobia, or other systems of domination promote, reinforce, or perpetuate harm and harming in our lives? How can we unlearn these old teachings?

We need to wake up and notice our relationships to others and our location in systems such as white supremacy so that we can unlearn harmful ones and intentionally relearn wholeness-based ones. We can't ignore it. To heal, we have to see where we've been a part of white supremacy culture and other systems of injustice, even perhaps where we've been complicit, intentionally or unintentionally, knowingly or unknowingly. I have to be open to the possibility that as an Asian American queer woman, I might unknowingly participate in anti-Blackness, ableism, or some other harm. We all have to fully acknowledge the ramifications of the impact of our location as it is and not as we want it to be.

We need to examine how we're taught that certain people's suffering matters while other people's suffering does not. For Asian Americans and other people of color, this often includes learning how we've internalized messages to dismiss our own experiences. My first reaction to a racist experience is often one of disbelief. I think to myself, "Did they really just say that? How can this be happening in this day and age?" These reactive thoughts are a subtle way to deflect and minimize my own experience. We need to understand how we've internalized racist messages that our suffering is not valid or important.

Classically, the practice instruction of the Second Noble Truth is "to abandon" or "let go." Abandoning is hard, especially around reactive, habitual patterns. For me, it's easier to let go of something when I know how uncomfortable it is or when I can see clearly how it's not working anymore. In doing so, I'm more able to live in the now from my own chosen values.

So much of Dharma practice is to learn to broaden our view so that we're looking at the context and not just the content. For example, in the summer of 2020, when the Black Lives Matter protests were going on all over the world, the reality that this was a structural issue could not be denied by dominant society any longer. Given this context, the Merriam-Webster dictionary changed its definition of racism to finally include systemic oppression after a young Black woman lobbied for it. While not a policy change, words reflect what's important in a culture. The woman who lobbied for this new definition contributed to all of us being able to change how we describe ourselves and our view of the world we live in, helping us "abandon" or "let go" of old frameworks.

I know that for me, what has been so difficult in my antiracist work has been to find common language with others, especially those in the up-power position. Back in the mid-2000s, a Dharma center I worked with asked me several times to start a weekly people-of-color (POC) meditation group, but I refused because, while they were interested in "bringing in more POC," I knew that the temple's almost exclusively white environment, especially in leadership staffing, would not be a supportive environment for POC. I said that I would not run such a group until the center committed to having white privilege and entitlement trainings. They took a brief time to do this training, but when the majority of senior staff never attended these trainings, and when there was a push to mentor and to provide senior staff positions to POCs as a form of including POCs in leadership or power-holding positions, that round of trainings was let go "due to budget issues." And thus, nothing changed much. In the years since, white privilege and entitlement trainings have now become mainstream for many white convert centers. However, the work of mentoring, training, and providing equitable teaching and leadership opportunities for BIPOC teachers remains minimal or is done in tokenistic ways. Additionally, even in their efforts to be more racially inclusive, Asian American presence and voices remain minimal or invisibilized.

For example, at a one-day POC retreat a while back, a non-Asian BIPOC teacher said that Buddhism came from the white teachers, like his own, who "brought it back from Asia." When my Chinese American friend voiced that her grandmother came to the United States around 1870 and was a Buddhist, his answer was, "That doesn't matter. That's not what I'm talking about." Buddhism came from India, from Asia, and has been practiced throughout Asia for over two and a half millennia. And things have not changed much because, just this year, at the same white-centered convert Buddhism meditation center, at a silent nine-day retreat I attended, a person in Q&A asked a Black teacher how come quietness and stillness were so emphasized in Buddhism. That teacher's go-to answer was essentially, "If it was a whole bunch of Black people who had gone to Asia to bring Buddhism back, you bet it would be a lot more singing and dancing!" To ignore the long history of Asian American heritage Buddhism in North America and simply adopt the white-centered convert Buddhist version and perspectives, and thus continuing to minimize, invisibilize, and erase Asian-heritage practitioners' presence and contributions, is to collude in the system of white supremacy through appropriation.

When we realize that what we've been taught no longer serves us or the communities we're part of or serve, it will hopefully inspire us to let go of old points of view, beliefs, and actions of body, speech, and mind that continue to not only misrepresent but also perpetuate hatred and violence in all its forms.

Racism is not a one-time event. No person experiences just one racially defining moment. Racism is a system of oppression, a manifestation of the system of white supremacy, and it affects us all. But conditions change. What was important and relevant to us in the past versus now needs to be examined and, when appropriate, adapted or changed. Practicing to abandon or let go of hurtful and harmful impacts is essential to individual and collective healing.

PRACTICE PAUSE

—— *Mindful Writing* ——

Letting Go of Old Beliefs Reflection

Think of and write a *minor* example (to be able to stay within your range of tolerance) of your racial conditioning that you can apply the following questions to:

- What one thing about this racial conditioning has been important to me up to this time?

- Is what has been important still in accordance with the current contexts of my life?

- If it's not, what *aspects* of how it was important no longer serve me or aren't in alignment with my values or aims anymore and need to be let go?

- How can I abandon or let it go?

- In what contexts can I let it go? (Letting go doesn't have to be all or nothing.)

How was it to answer these questions for yourself? I hope taking this pause to reflect on these questions supports you to clarify how you were taught or conditioned in ways that are no longer helpful or in accordance with your values now and, in doing so, supports you to align or realign yourself to what's important to you now to have, or reconnect to, a sense of wholeness.

Engaged Third Noble Truth
Individual and Collective Agency for Ending Harm Is Possible

Next we focus on what I call liberatory agency: responding in body, speech, and mind with mindful intention or motivation instead of reactivity. Classically, the Third Noble Truth is described as "there is an end to suffering." With the Engaged Third Noble Truth, we focus on the possibility for agency, especially in the midst of harm and difficulty. How can we find grounding and spaciousness in the midst of oppressive systems? Instead of reacting, how can we respond with wise, skillful choices and actions? Conditions can change and we can be a part of it.

What we think and how we behave has an impact on our internal wellness and reverberates out to our families, communities, nation, and the earth itself. We can come home to ourselves—to heal ourselves—by identifying how we can respond differently to harm. How can we unlearn the ways we were taught to react to harm and relearn ways to act from a sense of wholeness? How can our responses encourage repair? Our answers to these questions are important and the quality of our responses are just as important.

In the teachings, *bodhicitta* is defined as "awakened heart-mind." What are we awakening to? We're awakening to the wholeness of full awareness and to sustaining this awareness. We're awakening to the trust and faith that wholeness is knowable and accessible to everyone. With bodhicitta, we awaken to the realization that we are stewards in repairing and recreating our full interconnections with each other. This is the beginning of restoration—to *know and live* from wholeness.

Bodhicitta practice, then, asks us to become aware of how we harm and how we are contributing to the causes of harm. Therefore, the practice instruction for the Third Noble Truth, "to realize," is to acknowledge how we have harmed ourselves or others and to understand the drive behind such behaviors *as a means to skillful restoration.*

This is vulnerability at work. "Realizing," in much of Buddhism, means to attain enlightenment, to fully know awakening. For me, the Engaged Third Noble Truth is about agency and being willing to fully embody the teachings of the Engaged Four Noble Truths. As applied to white supremacy culture, this means we fully acknowledge the causes and impacts of harm and harming, how we have colluded or contributed to it, and how we can heal from it.

With the Engaged Third Noble Truth, we move from acting out the ideas and behaviors we inherited to asking ourselves how we can think, act, and interact from wholeness. We move from learned, fragmenting notions of who or what deserves consideration and move toward taking responsibility for our own and collective actions and the impacts they have. From the old conditioning of centering individualism, where our mistrust has each of us thinking about our own piece of the pie, we can shift our focus to realizing, engaging, and stewarding a collective wholeness. We can ask, How can this be a home for all beings?

If this sounds overwhelming, don't worry or despair! Eihei Dogen, the founder of Soto Zen, coined the phrase "practice-realization," which means *in* the doing *is* the realization. To be antiracist isn't to read about it or think about it, we have to actively enact antiracism. Engaging in antiracist work and movements is building a home for all beings.

Engaged Fourth Noble Truth
The Eightfold Path Empowers Wholeness

The last of the Four Noble Truths is the Eightfold Path. The classic version simply states that the Path is the way to end suffering. The Engaged Eightfold Path version offers a more uplifting and direct aim of practice: We are empowered for individual healing and systemic restoration to wholeness.

These eight factors offer us ways to respond to harm with our mind, heart, and body and come home to wholeness. The Engaged Eightfold Path is restorative, providing instructions and practices to *prevent us* from being part of conditions that promote harm, guiding us in *healing* from harm we've experienced, and *rectifying* harm we've caused. It gives us aspirational values to connect us to our innate wholeness and it provides us with clear, skillful ways to return to our individual and collective wholeness, especially when we've experienced dukkha or harm. The beauty of the Engaged Eightfold Path is that we are given clear ways to practice with each factor so that they are not just concepts to memorize but qualities and skills to develop.

Each factor of the Eightfold Path was originally translated as "right," as in Right View or Right Living. I've heard this kind of "right" explained as the "right" way to milk a cow. You can't go and pull on any part of the cow. There's one "right" place to get milk. To me this is about appropriateness and it makes sense. However, as the word *right* often brings up its binary of *wrong*, and thus an associative sense of judgment, I've chosen to use the word *skillful* because it connotes both *knowing* what's skillful and *practicing* to be skillful. Hopefully, this will also support us as practitioners to know that the Engaged Eightfold Path is a set of developmental practices versus setting them up as simply tasks to be checked off as having achieved or failed. Additionally, I'm presenting them in an order that I hope will build trust and confidence that these practices can help us all come home to the wholeness of life. They are Skillful: View, Concentration, Motivation, Effort, Mindfulness, Speech, Enacting, and Living.

Each factor of the Eightfold Path promotes nonharming and is delineated into one of three groupings: wisdom, ethical conduct, or meditative. Like the Engaged Four Noble Truths, I've reframed these fundamental teachings to be inclusive of the personal and the structural, providing us with teachings and practices that are tangible and meaningful in the complexity of our contemporary lives, especially when impacted by the system of white supremacy and other injustices. In subsequent chapters of this book, we'll see how the Engaged Eightfold Path outlines concrete skills to develop and how it offers meditative practices to restore and heal from the deep wounds of racism.

- **Skillful View** begins our journey on the Path by reconnecting to and building confidence in the wholeness of our interconnection as a way to practice with the Engaged Four Noble Truths while acknowledging how the karmic seeds of racism were planted.

- **Skillful Concentration** is a meditative practice that can help us understand the layers of our racial conditioning in the system of white supremacy, supporting us to be centered instead of overwhelmed by our own or the suffering of the world.

- **Skillful Motivation** shows us that there's choice, or agency, in our field of awareness by accessing and cultivating qualities of goodwill, compassion, inclusive joy, and equanimity so that our motivations are in congruence with wholeness.

- **Skillful Effort** gives us clear guidance with the Four Instructions and the Five Hindrances as ways to work with difficulties and to respond from wholeness within a clear framework of what's skillful and what's not.

- **Skillful Mindfulness** will give us the wherewithal to know and act with liberatory agency instead of reactivity to our racial conditioning, to shift our life from just surviving to centering how we can thrive in wholeness.

- **Skillful Speech** recenters the aim of communications to wholeness, from an overfocus on individualistic and divisive speech to context and connection.

- **Skillful Enactment** offers guidance with the Compassionate Connection precepts as a rudder and for actualizing our nonharming commitments in everyday life and collective activism.
- **Skillful Living** is the commitment to bring all that we've discovered on the Path to foster wholeness and nonharming from this day forth.

○ ○ ○ ○

The day after that mind-stopping meeting in Japan, Sekkei Harada Roshi offered me another chance for a dokusan interview. I rang the bell, did my bows, and went into the practice discussion room, ready to share my insights about how his answer had affected me. Before I could open my mouth, Roshi launched into a lengthy story of Shakyamuni Buddha's life and enlightenment along with the histories of other early Buddhist ancestors. Then, once again, he rang me out of the room.

We never spoke about my question again.

This event impacted me deeply and I continued to turn it over for many years afterward. When I remember my dokusans with Sekkei Harada Roshi, this last part has always puzzled me. I often wondered, what was his point about it all? In writing this now, I have an understanding of what he was teaching me. The Buddha and ancestors were searching for the same things as you and me: an end to suffering.

I think Roshi was saying that there can't be spiritual bypass. He realized—and after that initial exchange I, too, realized—that I was looking for a way to explain away the hurt and pain by wanting to discuss it. Discussion isn't wrong. Theory isn't wrong. Activism isn't wrong. But we can't use these things for spiritual bypass. We can't use Buddhist practice, or any methods such as race theory or activism, as a way to skip over the human condition inherent in the First Noble Truth—experiencing the hurts and pains of our lives. Trying to get away from them via any method is to try and skip over, or bypass, fully experiencing our life as-it-is. Our practice *is* to get closer and closer to "know it completely" because, in doing so, we can actually then have more clarity on how we can heal. In Pali, the first recorded language of Buddhism, the term *yoniso manasikara* is usually translated as "wise attention." It can also be translated as "attention that takes the whole into account."[1] This is what Sekkei Harada Roshi was pointing me toward: the practice of investigating dukkha, which sees it in context, in totality, and not just the hurt and pain of the moment.

Then, the rest of the Engaged Four Noble Truths offer us descriptions and practices for how to connect or reconnect to the wholeness of life—that our existence is seen, relevant, healable, and valued—when we remember and access the contexts that validate us and support us to thrive. Additionally, we need to remember that *all beings* want the same thing: to be free from suffering and the causes of suffering. This is what connects us all.

Denying that systems of oppression exist is to deny reality as-it-is. Learning to negotiate these systems with self- and collective-determined agency is the practice of engaged liberation. In practicing collective liberation, this is what I wish for us: that we may come home to a sense of wholeness grounded in what is safe and of value to all. May we then aspire to spread that out, to work together to strengthen safety and care for each other. This is the work, and the liberation, of understanding, practicing, and developing the Engaged Four Noble Truths.

SKILLFUL VIEW
Transforming Past Seeds
into Future Wholeness

WHEN I WAS IN my late teens riding my bike to swim practice in a small college town in North Dakota, a car suddenly swerved up very close to me. As I wobbled on my ten-speed to adjust, a guy stuck his head out of the passenger window and yelled, "Hey, Chink! Go home!"

I looked behind me and didn't see anyone. I thought, "Who is he talking to? I'm not Chinese!"

As I turned back to face the car, it sped off, leaving a trail of derisive laughter behind.

That's when I realized he was talking to me.

As the car sped away, a wave of shame came over me that was a mixture of the pain and sadness of being ridiculed and the shame of being confused. Even today, I often find confusion is mixed in with other feelings when I've been a target of discrimination or racism. I'm left confused because I was being myself, being in my own space, my own life, and suddenly the wholeness of being perfectly in the midst of belonging to life is torn by hatred.

This incident happened in the early 1980s after I had moved from Cairo, Egypt, to this small predominantly white Midwestern town. My father had recently left the U.S. State Department to work at the local state college. Since my adoption at the age of eight from Vietnam, I had lived mostly overseas in American embassy communities. In Egypt I spent my weekdays going to the expat Cairo American College and weekends playing Marco Polo in the embassy's swimming pool. We had diplomatic passports and traveled extensively throughout Europe, Africa, and the Middle East. Everywhere I went, I was fully identified as American, often in revered ways, such as being able to go through special lines at airports and then picked up and motored off by hired drivers.

Perhaps it was because I wasn't born in the United States and had never lived in such a predominantly white town until then, but I had never experienced directed hatred like this before. This incident showed me that no matter how I viewed myself, others viewed me differently, and sometimes that view was filled with contempt.

○ ○ ○ ○

The Engaged Eightfold Path offers steps to understand, practice, and realize the completeness of our human life. It gives us direct ways to live with wisdom, nonharming, and wholeness through cultivating meditative and mindful practices. Because we need to see ourselves and the world clearly in order to engage with our practice in a meaningful way, Skillful View is where the Eightfold Path begins. Skillful View and Skillful Motivation are the two factors that make up the Wisdom grouping of the Eightfold Path.

To practice Skillful View is to learn to shift our perception so we can *understand* and *be with* harm and harming—our own, that of others, and the world's—in service of healing and restoration. Skillful View can help us stop turning away from suffering because we're overwhelmed, and instead learn ways to view or understand it more skillfully.

Part of this shift is to learn to reframe the process of observation itself. In my teaching I explain this shift to my students as moving "from cage to container." This means that I practice to shift from understanding my life as a cage—that things are being done to me—to understanding my life as a container—that there's support and safety in life. I do this to transform my life from just surviving the traumas of chronic oppressions to a life grounded in joyful thriving, in wholeness. From fearful cage to joyful container.

To help you investigate this, you can ask yourself, How am I part of the whole of life instead of an object being acted upon? In other words, How can I transform my view of life being done *to* me to how I am *in* life? Going even deeper, you can ask yourself, How can I know I have agency in the midst of oppressive systems of domination? How can I live with mindful agency instead of reactivity?

PRACTICE PAUSE

—— *Mindful Writing* ——

Readying to Move from Cage to Container

As is true for any of these Practice Pauses, in general, pick a mild example, especially if it's your first time doing this exercise. In particular around racialization and racism, it's highly suggested to *not* use a race-based example at first.

To help you investigate this concept of moving from cage to container, you can ask yourself:

- How can I know I'm part of the whole of life?

- In what circumstances have I felt like an object being acted upon?

- In this situation, how can I activate self-agency to transform this view?

- In doing so, what lets me know I am *in* life?

- How can I connect with another person or community that shares these values?

If using a race-based example:

- In terms of racism, how can I know I have agency in the midst of oppression?

When we've been in or are currently in chronic trauma, such as the hatred of white supremacy culture, part of its impact is to produce in us a lack of the sense of future, and with it, a lowered sense of self and collective agency that are *in service of thriving*. Thus, part of our healing and restoration is to reconnect and build confidence in how we do have a right to a future. We can have a future in which we have voice and agency, one in which we are part of its cocreation.

The answers to these questions will arise out of how we learn to understand and work with the other Engaged Noble Truths in general and, in particular, the Engaged Eightfold Path of the Fourth Noble Truth. The answers to these questions will be revealed as you read, study, and apply the teachings. Thus, as you read through this book, remember that the Practice Pauses will engage you in ways to apply the teachings.

LIBERATORY VIEWS

The teachings around Skillful View give us two ways to practice liberation. One way is by understanding the Four Noble Truths. As we saw in the last chapter, the Engaged Four Noble Truths are a framework to understand harm and harming. In summary, with the Engaged First Truth, we're shown how to clearly know harm and harming. With the Second, understanding the Four Noble Truths supports the realization of the causes and conditions for how harm and harming happen to individuals and communities, especially through systems. Third, they show us that harm and harming can end through individual and collective agency. And with the Fourth, we're shown that practicing the Eightfold Path empowers wholeness.

The second way to practice Skillful View is by understanding karma. *Karma* literally means "action." However, in Buddhism, our actions have some preceding cause, so a better definition is "volitional action," or the product of one's intention, aim, or motivation. The simplest way to understand karma is as the *process* of cause and effect. Put another way, every "action" of body, speech, and mind has a result. Past actions bring about current results, experienced in the present. Current motivations and the actions that stem from them prime future results. A cause brings about an effect, which becomes the cause for another effect, and so on.

In the teachings, the image of seeds in a field offers a way to understand karma and how it works. The kinds of seeds that are in the field are based on causes from the past. Certain seeds are more likely to sprout than others due to present conditions, such as how much rain and sun the field receives. I like to think of "volitional action" as the free will each person has to respond to the seeds that are already in their garden, as well as the free will each person has to respond to or add to the present conditions affecting their garden. For instance, a wise vegetable gardener knows what tomatoes need and so will plant seeds in a sunny spot. However, as any gardener knows, if you plant a seed, you're not necessarily going to get an exact kind of plant shown on the seed packet or any description you've read about the plant. There are many factors that will influence the plant's size, strength, longevity, or even color. With tomatoes, they like sun, but if it's also being planted in a very hot climate, a dappled shade spot may be best.

This is true in life as well. Karma isn't as simple and direct as A leads to B which leads to C. There are many causes and conditions, so we can't always know what will impact future results. In a way, then, this is a kind of not-knowing. We can settle into this not-knowing as a practice of focusing more on the possibilities for interconnection, the force that shows us wholeness. When we shift into living life in wholeness, we are aware that our current actions, especially when we act with positive, nonharming motivations, will more likely result in positive, nonharming outcomes. Thus, we can see that the willingness to be motivated by kindness and to act from goodwill, when based on a pure freely given desire to stop contributing to harm and harming, can propel us to live and act in wholeness, seeding more wholeness endlessly.

Our practice is to become *aware of how we harm and how we are contributing to the causes of harm.* Harm and harming are embedded in oppressive systems, but people can change, and these systems can end.

Achieving this awareness is challenging because it asks us to be with the impact of harm on ourselves and others. To become aware of how we harm and are contributing to the causes of harm, we can start by understanding our own suffering. I have formulated two ways to work with Skillful View to reframe our perceptions of suffering so we can stay open as we look closely at our own suffering and develop wisdom about the nature of suffering: the Reduction and the Dilution Methods.

The Reduction Method

One way to apply Skillful View as a way to work with dukkha is by what I call the Reduction Method. Imagine that our suffering was like a chunk of salt the size of a gumball. If we popped it in our mouth as-is, it would be extremely intense and unpleasant. But what if we broke it down into small chunks, reducing it to small sprinkles that could go on a tomato? That would be a much easier way to work with our suffering.

To practice the Reduction Method, we can meditate or engage in other Buddhist reflective practices such as chanting or reciting mantras. We could do mindful journal writing. Other practices could include mindful eating or mindfulness while doing the dishes. These practices give us a "container" to pay attention to more specific and subtler "chunks," or aspects, of our suffering. They can provide us with the meditative space to become aware of all our various reactions to harm and harming, and we may even start to see them in a sequence or pattern.

Whatever karmic seeds have come to me, I have the responsibility to include their impacts into what and how I choose my next intention and action. This is a practice to open me up to living with karma as a container and not as a cage.

PRACTICE PAUSE

One-Pointed Concentration Breath Meditation

Let's put the Reduction Method into practice with a very basic form of one-pointed breath meditation. We'll focus on paying attention to breathing in and out, a practice that is said to be the first meditation instructions given by the Buddha.

Take a comfortable and settled position. Close your eyes or keep them just slightly looking down if this helps you to focus.

Begin by paying attention to the breath.

First, notice when you're breathing in, noticing the sensation of the air as it enters your body as you take in a breath. However you feel it is fine.

Do this for three breaths.

Next, steady your focus on a location where you feel the air of the inhale as it enters: perhaps just above your lips or entering through your left or right nostril, or both. There's no right or wrong spot. What is key is being aware of the sensations of the movement of air as you inhale. And, if you can't feel it with this inhale, there'll be another, so you can let go if any anxious thoughts arise about doing it right or wrong. You can simply come back to focusing on being aware of the air's movement with the next inhale.

Do this for three breaths.

Now notice the beginning, middle, and end of an inhalation. Perhaps above your lips, then the left nostril, then the back of your throat. Again, if you notice only one or two spots only at first, that's fine. On each successive inhale, let yourself notice more and more the full pathway of the air as it enters.

Now do the same with the exhale, noticing first just one point and then adding the three locations.

Do this for three exhales or as long as is comfortable.

Open your eyes if they are closed.

In the Reduction Method, by focusing our awareness on a smaller area or at a subtler level, we often realize that we usually don't *just* pay attention to our breathing. Thoughts and emotions start to come up. Perhaps it's something like asking yourself, Should my breath be deeper? This question may cause us to feel anxious because our breath doesn't seem deep enough. Then we may become doubtful. Can I do this? Is this the right kind of meditation for me? Perhaps we'll even become so anxious and doubtful that we get up from our meditative position and give up!

With this one-pointed breath meditation, we're asked to keep coming back to notice the breath and to practice leaving the evaluative thoughts alone. We are encouraged to just start again each time we notice another thought, emotion, or mental activity that takes us away from *just* paying attention to the breath coming in and out. If thoughts come up about what the quality of the breath "should be," just let them come up and then let them go. Over and over again. This is the practice.

As we do this, concentration strengthens and settledness builds. When we activate Skillful Effort by coming back to just breathing, we build the foundation to be able to more clearly identify actual sensations, emotions, and thoughts in the moment, and see how they interact with each other. This then gives us a better understanding of how to work with them. For instance, as awareness builds through ongoing practice, we can notice that the breath most often tends to become shallower with anxious thoughts. So, when we're able to come back to just breathing, our breath will likely settle down and naturally become deeper, and our anxiety will also likely lessen.

Meditation like this is a form of the Reduction Method at work, breaking down our experience into parts so that we can know our experience, such as when we're suffering more clearly in body, heart, and mind at any given moment. This way we have more choice in how to attend to the ways we've been impacted by a harmful event such as a discriminatory or racist incident. For instance, when there's anxiety or fear, having practiced various forms of the Reduction Method, I know that I tend to hold my breath. Holding my breath stiffens my chest and shoulders, increasing the tension I'm feeling at such moments. Now that I've practiced with noticing sensations more, I'm able to have intentional agency to take a deep breath or two in such moments of distress. This provides me a grounding settledness to access with clarity what's going on inside and outside at the moment, and then, how to best attend to myself, another, or the situation at hand.

In the "Go home!" incident above, if I had such a meditative tool as a resource, I might have been able to attend to the fear I experienced when that car swerved so close to me. Instead, most of my memory of the experience is based on the shame of being laughed at and the confusion I felt as the result of the threat.

The Dilution Method

The other way to look closely at our suffering is the Dilution Method. To do this, we can go back to the image of the big chunk of salt, but this time we can put it into a pot of soup. In the soup, it wouldn't be such an overwhelming or unpleasant taste. Again, this is another way to make it easier to work with our suffering.

The Dilution Method is inherent in Buddhist wisdom practices as we are continuously asked to open up our view. The beliefs and views we have now are the result of how we were conditioned. These are the karmic results of past motivations and actions that we've inherited. Our practice is to learn to bring awareness to what those messages were and whether they're still useful or skillful in our present circumstances. This is the key to how we can use the Engaged Four Noble Truths throughout this book. Bringing in a systemic lens to investigate how we were conditioned to be with our internal experiences and how we were taught to react to external situations is a form of the Dilution Method. When we open up our view to how our individual experience is within larger contexts, such as historical, cultural, and other systemic processes, it can often allow for healing as our individual experience is held in larger contexts, showing us the nonpersonalness of our experience. While the experience of being the target of hatred such as racism is significantly painful personally, when I view it as part of a larger category or social location, I am reminded that my suffering, like a gumball-size salt rock, is held in the ocean, the net, of others with the same experience. For me, this context activates my agency to give back, to make use of my suffering in a way that will help everyone. Then, my suffering will have been of meaning, and I have more understanding of suffering and how it can end. This is the essence of the Dilution Method.

There's an intense famous story about the Dilution Method in the sutras, collections of Buddhist teachings. Kisagotami was a woman whose son had died. She was distraught to the point of senselessness, asking everyone for medicine for her son even though he had passed. Someone directed her to the Buddha. She went, carrying her son's corpse, asking the Buddha to cure him. The Buddha, assessing the situation, said that he had medicine but that she would have to do one thing first: bring back a mustard seed from a house that had never experienced death. Kisagotami readily agreed. She went to visit every house in the village, asking each for this. At each house, she was met with the same answers: "yes" to giving her mustard seeds but "no" to the fact that their household had not experienced any death. As she continued on her quest, she began to understand the impersonal nature of death. When she returned to the Buddha without any mustard seeds, he sang her a verse about the universality of death. Upon hearing it, she attained enlightenment.

Kisagotami realized that her grief for her son, while deep and intense personally, was also a part of the larger structure of impermanence: death will affect all of us, in every family. Our individual pain *can* be held by the collective experience. The collective perspective provides the remembrance of the net as being the support for each and every jewel. And thus, as we attend to the net, we attend to the lives of every jewel. This is the support offered by the Dilution Method.

○ ○ ○ ○

"Abandoning" is the classic word for the practice instruction of the Second Noble Truth. To me, "abandoning" can sound too clear cut; like I "should" just now be able to abandon something because I understand it more, especially as a thought or concept. I think it's more approachable to remember that "letting go" is another word for it.

To work with racism, the Dilution Method supports us to practice so that we are able to let go of thoughts and emotions that promote hate, greed, and ignorance as they foster behaviors that cause harm to ourselves and others. Bringing in the context of history in our family, culture, political movements, or other societal events around a memory or experience of racialization or racism is a powerful way to practice the Dilution Method. For instance, when remembering or experiencing a racist event, I often find myself wondering why I've been targeted or how people can be so racist. Understanding the history of time and place in which that memory or event happened can give contextual answers, often bringing with it an alleviation of the sense that it's simply personal, supporting the release, or letting go, of some or all of the resulting harm it has caused.

From our understanding of karma, we know that racism doesn't come from nowhere. In the United States there's a long history that created conditions for my bike incident to happen. Why this man chose to yell out a belligerent epithet at me is based on a long history of white supremacy culture in the United States, a history that stretches back to colonialism that brought untold violence to the Indigenous peoples of North America, and that planted seeds for a mindset that uses hatred and violence against other people—in this case, an immigrated Vietnamese American adoptee like me.

I don't know why that man chose to yell the slur "chink" at me, but I do know that slur is almost 150 years old. Throughout history, Asian immigrants and Asian Americans have been lumped together by white supremacy and incorrectly seen as interchangeable. Chinese immigrants were some of the first to come from Asia to the United States. The Chinese American experience reveals how this history of white supremacy has impacted all Asian Americans.

Beginning in 1849, Chinese people came to California to seek their fortunes during the gold rush, calling this land "Gold Mountain." As more people started coming from all over the world, including China, white miners became resentful. The Foreign Miners' Tax Act of 1850[1] and the Foreign Miners' License Tax Act of 1852 were specifically aimed at Chinese miners as well as miners from Latin America. Foreign miners from Ireland, England, and Germany and white miners from Canada protested against the tax and were given exemptions as "free white persons."[2]

From 1863 to 1869, American companies actively recruited people from China to work on the Transcontinental Railroad. Brought by "credit money," these workers essentially became indentured servants as they struggled to pay back the fees. Many ended up staying in the United States as they could never afford the fare to return to China. Then, as their labor was no longer needed, animus rose, and people of Chinese ancestry were called the "Yellow Peril."

Discrimination and anti-Chinese violence grew. One such event was the Los Angeles massacre of 1871 in which seventeen Chinese people were hanged, the largest lynching in U.S. history. Research on that massacre also shows that it involved cover-ups by many city officials, so the full story was not known until recently, when an *LA Weekly* freelance reporter brought it to national attention.[3]

The Page Act of 1875 specifically excluded East Asian women from entering the United States, stereotyping them as prostitutes. Then in 1882, the Chinese Exclusion Act essentially ended immigration of people from China.[4] Such incidents demonstrate how xenophobia and racism became systemized into laws.

Even though none of us were alive during that time, this history still impacts us today. It impacted me as a Vietnamese American teen riding my bike.

In the years since the war with Vietnam, many Vietnamese people have immigrated to the United States. The years 1978 and 1979 saw the largest influx of Vietnamese refugees, and media coverage of them as "boat people" was pervasive. A large number were sponsored by Christian groups in the Midwest, so many came to live in Minneapolis, not too far from where I lived and rode my bike.

At the same time, Japanese car imports were becoming more popular, highlighting problems that had been evident in the American Big Three automakers for some time and which caused significant layoffs in Detroit. The layoffs were blamed on Japan, and anti-Asian racism surged. Even though anti-Asian racism at this time was focused on Japan, the white supremacist notion that "all Asians are the same" meant that anyone could be in danger. In 1982, Vincent Chin, a Chinese American man, was killed in Detroit by two white men, Ronald Ebens, a Chrysler plant supervisor, and his stepson Michael Nitz, who had been laid off from his auto-work job. The men denied that they were motivated by race, were given a $3,000 fine on manslaughter charges, and served no time in jail.[5]

Buddhist settings are also affected by this history of white supremacy. For instance, not long ago I was at a Dharma talk at a well-known predominantly white convert Buddhist center. The Abbot said, more than once, "Buddhism came to America some forty-nine or fifty years ago." While it was his attempt to pay homage to the Asian founder of that convert lineage, those comments were a form of erasure, leaving out the history of Buddhism in the United States practiced by Asian immigrants and their communities going back generations. In fact, the founder of his lineage was invited to the United States by a Japanese American community to lead their almost hundred-year-old temple as they were still working to recover from being forced into internment and concentration camps during World War II.

With that one sentence, the Abbot erased the lives of all early Asian-heritage Buddhists immigrants. Records of Japanese and Chinese immigrants who were Buddhists started in the middle of the nineteenth century. In San Francisco's Chinatown alone, there were eight Buddhist temples by 1875.[6] Additionally, most Asian Buddhist teachers did not come to start predominantly white convert Buddhist centers or organizations. Most were sponsored by their own ethnic-heritaged community to lead their specific ethnic-heritaged congregation. White practitioners came later, sometimes at a loss to Asian American communities, as their teachers could be drawn away by the needs of these later practitioners.

This is an example of how we can see that the Abbot's racist comment, while hurtful to the lineage, is also just one of many beliefs and acts of erasure through white supremacy machination and conditioning. The Dilution Method offers us a way to see our individual experience in context of a larger systemic force.

For me, the Dilution Method offers healing and restoration because it has helped me to see the impersonal nature of other people's behavior. In a paradoxical way, by seeing the context of a person's behavior or an organization's policies, or lack thereof, to be part of a larger system that has taught them to be that way tends to take away the sting that it is purely an individual act toward me. For me, when I can see that when I have behaved unskillfully, it is because of how *a whole system* that includes family, culture, the education system, government, and so on taught me to behave. When I realize that I didn't know better because I had not been trained to question the behavior, that opens up the space for me to realize that I can unlearn and relearn. Having this perspective offers us all a compassionate way to meet how we've hurt and harmed, individually and collectively.

Opening up our view to a larger perspective gives us an understanding that there are bigger forces at play, taking away some of the personal shame or guilt that may come with knowing we haven't acted from our best selves, from a sense of connection and wholeness. When I'm aware of that for myself, I'm more likely to acknowledge these larger forces are operating with others also, thus reducing my tendency to judge others for their unskillful behavior. Thus, the Dilution Method actually reminds us that there are many causes and conditions at play, and hence racism and any of the other isms, while done and felt by individuals, are actually habitual tendencies, which is one way I'd define karma. We can either continue these tendencies, or, if we're willing and able to bring awareness to them, we can stop such thoughts and behaviors. Learned hatred can end when we're aware of it and are able to transform it.

APPLYING THE SKILLFUL VIEW METHODS

To see how the Reduction and Dilution Methods could work with an experience of racism, let's take the incident when I was on my bike as an example.

The Reduction Method is especially useful because it supports us to clearly know our experience as habitual tendencies, or conditioned karmic loops. During a racist incident, we're conditioned to frame our experience mentally. Think about it. Most often around such incidents, the first question we are asked is "What happened?" Rarely are we asked, "How are you? Are you okay?"

It's also typical of a trauma response to focus and perseverate on the mind's narrative. We often try to make sense of what's happening with our thinking even though our bodies and emotions are in more immediate danger. That fast-moving car pulled up very close to me, so physical danger was present. Fear was also present. However, my first reaction when that act of violence was being directed at me was to think to myself, "Who is he talking to? I'm not Chinese!" We often focus on the content and don't remember to attend to the full context of an event. The three meditative qualities of Skillful Effort, Mindfulness, and Concentration of the Engaged Eightfold Path, when practiced diligently, support and strengthen our ability to skillfully discern all the various happenings in body, emotion, and mind so that we can increase our ability to attend to them better.

For me and the above memory, the Dilution Method came about in two ways. As I shared earlier, I was adopted by white parents. They were much older, a product of the pre–Civil Rights era and conditioned not to talk about race and racism. I wasn't raised to frame my race-based experience in a larger context than just personal.

Secondly, it took going away to college in Oregon, where I took many classes and finally minored in ethnic studies. That's when I first understood that the system of white supremacy and anti-Asian racism resulted in the microaggressions and violence toward me as a Vietnamese American. I also learned that healing from racialization and racism is an act of resistance. It's a way to stop colluding with white supremacy culture's promotion and enforcement of a constricted and fractured experience for me and other people of color.

Additionally, my many professors, teacher's assistants, and friends from the university's ethnic studies and anti-apartheid movement were a community in which I could relearn a more whole view of myself. My healing began when I could understand how the racist experiences directed at me were part of a larger structure *and* feel that the harms of racism could be addressed as part of collective political action. This, along with other engagements in collective activism in the realm of gender, sexual orientation, immigration, class, and other issues, has redirected old hurts and harms to a dedication to ending harm and harming while promoting wholeness and interconnectedness.

This, for me, is healing from the harm of racism. From this commitment, I can be more whole and complete, knowing that wholeness is possible and true. And if it's true for me, then it can be true for others also. It can be true for all beings.

○ ○ ○ ○

I never told anyone of that "Go home" incident, in part because I had no framing to understand the context of systemic racism until I went to college and took ethnic studies a few years later. Given the fact that my parents were white and didn't have a sense of race consciousness, and the fact that this was the Midwest in the 1980s, I understood this situation and others like it as people being mean to me, and I didn't understand why. I had no frame of reference to help me view this in a different way.

While this memory can still bring up a sense of fear and trepidation for me anytime I remember it, when I'm mindful, I clearly know that these feelings are old, and that currently I am not being threatened, and that I'm safe. It's as if there's a cut on your hand that hasn't healed; every time something touches it, due to the tenderness of the wound site, it hurts even more or can reopen. We have to attend to it to let it heal fully. With such awareness that I'm safe in the present moment, I am attending to old harm. Such healing can support being able to respond with more in-the-moment agency when I am being physically threatened or being the target of microaggressions in the moment. For instance, I have been called "chink" and told to "go home" many times since that incident. Instead of confusion, these days, if I answer at all, it would immediately be with "I am home!" or "This is my home!"

As Asian Americans or people of color, it's important that each of us heals on a personal level from being targets of hatred and racist violence. We also need to apply Skillful Effort to understanding, rectifying, and overcoming harm and harming to all the other social locations in the system of white supremacy, as racism impacts us all. This is true for other systemic injustices as well. Antiracism is everyone's practice, and it's connected to other oppressive systems. A life of wholeness includes all.

With Skillful View, we're given the Engaged Four Noble Truths and karma as a framework for seeing how our personal experiences of the impact of white supremacy culture comes into being both individually and in collective contexts. Broadly, we could say that the Reduction Method supports identifying and building the capacity to be with our memories or current experiences by viewing them in smaller and smaller and subtler and subtler "chunks" that make them manageable. The Dilution Method offers us an opening-up of our views to support knowing how events truly are conditioned by larger systemic forces. Thus, they offer us ways to regulate how we can use relative and absolute to support us to negotiate the challenges of our lives.

"The Middle Way," as Buddhism is often called, is not some "place" per se. It's the freedom of knowing that our lives are the negotiation between relative and absolute; not to be stuck in one or the other point of view. Thus, Skillful View is being open to all views of how harm and harming comes into being and how it can end. The Engaged Skillful View reminds us to be inclusive: to make sure all beings know Skillful View as innate. It can heal us from old hateful beliefs and actions that fragment us from this knowing. We need to make sure knowing Skillful View and its intertwining other factors of the Eightfold Path are available to all.

SKILLFUL CONCENTRATION
The Groundedness of Letting Go

IT WAS WINTER at the monastery in Central California where I had been practicing for almost two years. We were in *sesshin*, a seven-day Soto Zen meditation intensive, and this one was during one of the monastic practice periods known as *ango* or "rain retreats." These retreats are based on the practice that the Buddha and his monastics did together during the Indian monsoon season, gathering from dispersed places to practice intensively together. During this monastery's six months of retreat, for one week each month, we meditated even more intensively, from 4 a.m. until 9 p.m. After more than two years of combined monastic living and these repeated retreats, I had a deep sense of groundedness and settledness achieved only through continuous concentration and mindfulness practice.

I was deep in the last days of our last sesshin, sitting in my assigned seat in the rectangular meditation hall that we call the *zendo*. The teacher was a very senior person at this temple who practiced closely with the Japanese founder of this lineage. He was white, as all the teachers had been thus far. He was giving a Dharma talk, a formal teaching, reading us a well-known koan from twelfth-century China.

Case 53: Once when Great Master Ma and Pai Chang were walking together, they saw some wild ducks flying by. The Great Master said, "What is that?" Chang said, "Wild ducks." The Great Master said, "Where have they gone?" Chang said, "They've flown away." The Great Master then twisted Pai Chang's nose. Chang cried out in pain. The Great Master said, "When have they ever flown away?"[1]

The teacher then paused. I held my breath, waiting for the commentary. Classically, when a teacher presents a koan, their commentaries on the case show their awakening and understanding on how it's to be applied to practice and to life. This was my first practice period with this teacher and he was, according to many people here, the most adept teacher of this lineage.

The teacher continued, "Zen Masters should carry a napkin. Get a better grip that way. Otherwise it slips off just when you're getting good traction. Chinese people don't have big noses either. You know they're kind of flat so they're not that easy to get a hold of, like a Greek or Roman nose."

Laughter erupted around me as he spoke, building to a crescendo.

As the laughter echoed, the zendo seemed to stretch far away from me. It didn't feel like I was leaving the zendo. Instead I felt like I was staying still in my seat and everyone in the room elongated *away from me.*

Then, I clearly heard these words in my head: "Ah. Other."

I had no contraction in my chest. I had no pain in my heart. I had no tightening of my throat. No stories came to me at all. I had often experienced emotional and physical pains from being othered as a Vietnamese American woman in the white supremacy culture of the United States. This time those pains were missing, leaving room for insight into the essence of things as they are.

Just a pure thought arose describing the experience: "Ah. Other."

Before this moment, I had a feeling of wholeness from being one with the group of listeners. Afterward, I could see how the teacher's words and the sangha's participation in the joke created separation. The insight I had was that othering is a process that arises from some drive when causes of harm are present and acted on. It was a clear example of how a racist incident plays out when everyone takes on their role as assigned by white supremacy culture. The teacher took his position, white privilege and entitlement conditioning providing the drive for him to think this was just a joke and it wasn't racist at all. Participants in the zendo took their location, laughing at a joke that they weren't able to acknowledge as racist.

After my insight that day, I understood that a racist incident is a moment in which white supremacist conditioning plays out. Each person involved acts out their conditioned location or role to perpetuate how the culture of white supremacy functions. In this case, the people involved were imputing racial constructs on each other and colluding and reinforcing these ideas.

Those who laughed colluded in his comments as a joke that stereotyped Asians as having flat noses and implied that Greek- or Roman-descended white noses are better. It isn't farfetched to hypothesize that if the room was filled with people of Asian heritage, that white teacher would never have made such a comment. He knew the people there would collude in white supremacy culture conditioning. However, at that moment I did not collude in white supremacy culture conditioning. I did not "take" my location in white supremacy; I clearly understood that I was not less-than, contrary to what was being implied in the teacher's comments.

I experienced something different at that moment. My mind diverted from its conditioned, habitual loop. After months of intense monastic, mindfulness, and meditative practices, I didn't respond to this racist story in the typical ways I had in the past. I realized that the system of white supremacy depended on me to internalize victimization as a person of Asian descent. White supremacy culture is strengthened when I internalize the othering as a sense of less-than, or "lack," in myself; that somehow "not belonging" was something that is just up to me to rethink or overcome. The incident helped me understand that what I normally saw as a personal lack in myself were really *causes and conditions* that removed me from the whole.

○ ○ ○ ○

Part of the machination of racism is the creation of white supremacy culture, and with it, the conditioning and enforcement for each race to inhabit and stay in a designated location in this system. A racist incident can only happen when two or more people are involved in participating within the established rules of white supremacy culture. Everyone involved is affected by such an event. The degree of consequence on each person in the incident varies relative to the privilege, or lack of privilege, they have in their prescribed racial location in the system of white supremacy.

These roles have been taught to us by our families, our teachers, our cultural or religious practices, societal norms, and government policies for many generations. Centuries of colonialism and white supremacy culture have centered white Europeans and marginalized others. The word *Oriental* exemplifies this in that it means East of Europe or the "Occident." Language shapes our perspective, and this is an example that shows Europe as the center and sets up Asia as diametrically opposed to it. Along with this positioning came stereotypes of the West as modern and advanced, with the East juxtaposed as backward and traditional, a belief that continues to this day. It is the same structure that passed the Chinese Exclusion Act in 1882, the first federal law to exclude a group of people from immigration into the United States. It was an act of othering Asians on policy, government, and societal levels.

An exchange I had with a white practitioner elucidates the karmic consequences of this white-centric history, an example of the insidiousness of white supremacy's normalization. When I lived at the monastery in Central California, I actively promoted racial justice trainings, bringing in an organization to do a series of workshops. In one workshop, a white man was very clear he did not understand why such events should take place. He voiced the popular white convert Buddhist view that having meditation groups for people of color and talking about racial division was not Zen practice because they are ways of reiterating a sense of self-identity instead of practicing nonself. The trainer exchanged a few words with him, but he remained firm in his conviction.

About five years later, he and I saw each other again. He sought me out one day to share how he now understood why we had been doing antiracist work at the monastery. In the years since that training, he had gone to live at another practice center. It was on the big island of Hawaii and was run by a Japanese American with ties to Japan, so the majority of the guests were from Japan. He said that one day, as he was sitting at the kitchen table for lunch, he realized that he was not part of the conversations going on around him. Looking up, he realized he was the only white person at the table and that only Japanese was being spoken. He shared that he felt left out at that moment, and then the memory of the exchange at the racial justice workshop had flashed before him. It was at that moment that he understood how white-centered his views had been. For him, it took being in a location on the margins and relating to a loss of belonging to experience an inkling of what Asian Americans and other people of color face daily.

ASIAN OTHERING

As shared in chapter 2, examining U.S. history shows how white supremacy culture locates Asian Americans in the system of racism. A more specific example to Buddhism can be seen in the ways Asian Americans have been represented by dominant culture in "Buddhism in America." There's been a long history of white Buddhists framing Buddhism in the United States as "two Buddhisms." Their take, broadly, is to differentiate "ethnic Buddhists" who are Asian and practicing "superstitious" Buddhism with only chanting and bowing, from white convert Buddhists who are more "modern" and "scientific."[2]

For Asian Americans, as a way to support our healing from internalizing racism and practice antiracism is to understand that the role of "other" is conditioned and, while we can't escape being part of white supremacy culture, we don't have to "take" our place in it. It is true that for Asian Americans and other BIPOCs the consequences of stepping out of our prescribed location in the system of white supremacy often brings harsher, even life-threatening consequences. It is central to antiracist work for all of us to question and know that we do have choice, or agency, to not be part of white supremacy culture. This is both individual and collective work.

In moments like the one in the zendo, when I saw how the process of racism was clearly being enacted, deep healing happened for me. The locations we've been taught to inhabit in the system of white supremacy do not have to define us. We are more than an appointed location in any system.

Reverend Ryo Imamura, an eighteenth-generation priest in the Jodo Shin sect, in a 1992 letter to the editor, challenged *Tricycle* magazine's founder Helen Tworkov's assertion that "Asian-American Buddhists . . . so far . . . have not figured prominently in the development of something called American Buddhism." Furthermore, Tworkov's incorrect assertions deeply influenced the view in the United States that Asian American practitioners were "ethnic Buddhists" and that "convert Buddhists" or "spokespeople for Buddhism in America have been, almost exclusively, educated members of the white middle class."[3] Like many Asian American Buddhists, I was riveted by The Angry Asian Buddhist's web blog as Aaron J. Lee (aka arunlikhati) took on the continued underrepresentation and invisibilizing of Asian Americans during the growing "mindfulness" movement from 2009–2017, during which Asian American practitioners were largely absent from Buddhist publications and Buddhist conferences.[4]

More recently, eight people were killed in a shooting that took place at two spas in Atlanta on March 16, 2021. Six of the people killed were Asian or Asian American women. Though the law enforcement authorities on the case said that the shooter wasn't motivated by race, using the lens of history, the racism and misogyny toward Asian women behind the shooter's actions that day are clear for many racial justice advocates.[5]

One of many responses was a Buddhist-based event organized by Funie Hsu, Chenxing Han, and Reverend Duncan Ryuken Williams called May We Gather.[6] Described as "a National Buddhist Memorial for Asian American Ancestors," it brought together a wide variety of Buddhist clergy from a wide range of lineages and heritages.* While sparked by the death of Yong Ae Yue, one of the women killed in the spa shooting, it also raised awareness of five other Asian American Buddhists since 1885 whose deaths were

---

* As such, the vast majority were of Asian heritage, so in watching it, I found myself saying out loud to myself, "*This* is 'American Buddhism!'"

also due to racial violence but had not had much notice in national media. What was especially poignant was a seventh memorial tablet created for "all beings who have lost their lives through racial and religious animus" whose names are not known due to the erasure of Asian American history.

This erasure is part of the way white supremacy culture formulates racism toward Asians and Asian Americans in the United States. To commemorate the seven-week mourning period that is a Buddhist tradition, they brought together a diverse group of Buddhist monastics from many traditions to recognize the history of deaths of Asian-heritage Buddhists due to racial violence that had not been acknowledged before.

The invisibilization of Asian Americans continues today. Take a look at any mainstream Buddhist periodical and you'll see that it's still predominantly populated by whites, especially in positions of power and in decision-making roles such as directors, editors, and scholars. When there is a focus on "inclusivity" and "diversity" in convert-Buddhist settings, it is mostly focused on including Black Buddhists. Numerous events in convert-Buddhist centers throughout North America "for BIPOCs" do not include Asian American teachers, or the numbers pale in comparison to other teachers. Even within "diversity" actions, Asians are still invisible.

While I acknowledge worldwide anti-Blackness and the intense history of large-scale slavery of Africans and Afro-Caribbeans in the United States, and I support uplifting all BIPOCs, it is especially paradoxical to those of us of Asian ancestry that the representation of Buddhism—which started in India and is a religion that is predominantly practiced by Asians throughout the world—minimalizes or invisibilizes us. This was certainly a large part of the reason for my writing of this book. While "Asian Americans" is a large category, and I cannot represent all "Asian Buddhists," this is an offering to raise the voices and visibility of Asians practicing Buddhism in our many ways.

KNOWING DUKKHA

In daily life, it isn't so easy to have the kind of insight into the process of othering that I experienced in the zendo. Most often, when experiencing a racist incident, a chain of strong reactions is set off. The racist event happening in the moment gets linked to other racist incidents from the past. With the trauma of repeated racist incidents, this chain reaction perseverates and becomes more and more embedded. At such times, I don't have the settledness of deep concentration, or *samadhi,* such as that moment in the zendo. I'm often overwhelmed, activating my habitual ways of reacting.

When I am overcome by a racist incident and experiencing dukkha, either from one in progress or from a memory of one, my most common reaction is to move away from the experience. Other times, it could be denying it or trying to figure out a "fix" to solve it or stop it from happening again. And yet, I know that a healing practice for me is to *know* dukkha *fully* before I can *do* something to respond to it. Recognizing dukkha and its impact has supported me to know how to attend to current and old hurts and pains. It has supported me to clean out deep wounds so that transformational healing can happen.

We're practicing to get to know suffering not because we're masochists or sadists, but to find ways to not continue or collude in suffering, for the sake of ourselves and others. How can we best address hurt or harm? To do this means we have to understand how hurt or harm is affecting us. Acknowledging hurt and harm as we're experiencing it currently is key.

PRACTICE PAUSE

Breaking Down Suffering: Meditation and Off-the-Cushion Mindfulness Exercise

If asked, "Do you want to know more about suffering?" many of us would emphatically say, "No!" It's because, for most of us, suffering is an overwhelming and monolithic mass of ideas, concepts, and stories that swirl round and round in our heads, like mice scurrying in a maze looking for a way out. As discussed previously, the Reduction Method of

breaking our experience down into small "chunks" gives us an opportunity to be with the experience in ways that make it more manageable.

While it takes diligent and sustained practice to know all our experiences with clear, precise awareness, here is a meditation and off-the-
cushion exercise that will give you a great start because it breaks suffering
down into three components of our human experience: thoughts, emotions, and sensations.

- Begin by taking an easeful position.

- Close your eyes if it helps you to concentrate.

- Now bring up an event that bothers you just a little bit. (Really, make
  it small!)

- Next, notice a thought you're having about the event and silently
  label it "thought."

- Then label with one word the quality of the thought; for instance,
  "judgment" or "anxious."

- Now, notice an emotion you're having about it and silently label it
  "emotion."

- Then do the same, labeling with one word the quality of that emotion;
  for example, if related to the example of judgment above, perhaps
  "shame," or with anxiety, "dread."

- Now, do the same with a "sensation" quality. If relating to shame,
  perhaps "tightness" in the stomach or "squeezing" at the throat.

- Now go back to the event. What is the valence, or positive or negative affective quality, of the event now?

The above meditation can help us begin focusing on different aspects
of our experience. Hopefully it has given you more precise information
about what's going on with you in the moment already. With more
information, we can more appropriately respond. For instance, when I
find myself feeling a bit irritated or not quite satisfied, I pause and do
this meditation. Oftentimes I find out that I'm experiencing the sensation of cold. When I don't notice or attend to it, I find that irritation

often arises. I then find something or someone to be irritated with instead of just attending to the sensation of coldness and putting on a sweater.

For me, knowing more about the quality of my thought or emotion gives me more grounding. Breaking down an experience into these three categories, or "chunks," diffuses the "bigness" of suffering for me so that I can build my capacity to be with it and to know it more completely.

Off-the-Cushion Mindfulness Exercise

A variation of this to try on in daily life:

- Whenever you're feeling a bit off at any time in your day, pause.

- Notice what's most "up," or present, in the moment and label it: thought, emotion, or sensation.

- If there's time, note the quality of the thought, emotion, or sensation.

With the information you've gathered, you now have an opportunity to attend to it with volition.

The *window of tolerance* is a term used to describe the range in which a person is able to be with difficult events, internally or externally. When a traumatic event happens, there's so much stimulus that it's too overwhelming to process fully in that moment. If the situation is physically, emotionally, or psychologically dangerous and safety must be found quickly, there often isn't time or space to process all the various factors of the event. High-crisis or traumatic events can also bring on survival modes such as flight, fight, freeze, fawn (to please), and flop (collapse), triggering bodily responses such as panic, anxiety, shutdown, or other ways that are difficult to be with and thus takes us away from the present. Such events, especially if repeated or persistent, such as systemically oppressive experiences or environments, can condition us to have a narrower range of tolerance.

Traumatic experiences threaten our sense of self individually or as a community. Working with such events can bring up questions such as: What did the trauma involve? Was it physically harmful? Emotionally? Psychically? Was it part of generational trauma? How we were taught to be with a traumatic event conditions us. Are we processing it as a passing event? Or is it unresolved and unprocessed, becoming unconscious patterns of thoughts, beliefs, and behavior?

Part of what can determine if a high-crisis event becomes traumatic or not is that at the time of the event, we didn't have the space, time, or appropriate support to deal with it. Similarly, when we are reexperiencing or trying to work with old trauma, such as in meditation retreats or other practice situations, the lack of appropriate support only perpetuates ongoing symptoms of trauma. Meditation and practices open us up to our whole life, past and present, joys and sorrows. This is why retreat and practice centers need to be able to provide a trauma-informed container.

We need appropriate means to process all the various levels of impact so that the event makes sense, then and now. For many, "making sense" is merely a rational or mental narrative: this happened, then that happened, then I did this or you did that. Conventional work with trauma is often mostly focused on verbally analyzing the event. This has its use, without a doubt. However, trauma is *not* just the mental narrative of what happens. It's also the impact on our bodies and emotions. After a high-crisis or traumatic exposure, perseverating on the event and its accompanying feelings is common, a looping flood of overwhelming details in body, emotions, and mind.

If we become more conscious of how we were *taught to react to the impact* of traumatic racist experiences, we can better evaluate whether old responses are still useful to us now. We need support to develop the skills to *fully be* with a racial memory and its corresponding emotions and body sensations. Some questions you can ask yourself are: Does the degree of fear I am feeling now correlate to the current condition? Is the reaction to run, fight, shutdown, or appease the response I want to enact right here and now? Reflecting on these questions can help us assess if our experience is an old reaction that is no longer necessary to hold onto in our current interaction with the person or situation that's actually in front of us.

Therefore, to fully process trauma, we need to learn to be with it.* The practice instruction for the First Noble Truth is to investigate dukkha. There are two main aims to our investigation. One is to be able to identify dukkha. The second is to build our capacity to be with dukkha.

BUILDING STABILITY

While all of the Eightfold Path supports us in being with dukkha, Skillful Concentration, being part of the Meditative grouping of the Eightfold Path, along with Skillful Effort and Skillful Mindfulness, is especially fundamental because it is the factor that defines and develops stability and groundedness. Skillful Concentration includes two forms of meditative development: one-pointed (as demonstrated in the breath meditation example in chapter 2) and the stages of the metaphysical states of the *jhanas,* which literally means "absorption."

While the full four levels of absorption of jhana development is part of this factor of the Eightfold Path, because full jhanas are most often only experienced while in long, deep retreats and with very specific meditation instructions, it isn't possible to cover them in this format. As we are discussing practice in daily life, the stability and groundedness that can be achieved with basic one-pointed concentration is enough to support us to process difficulties that affect us in body, heart, and mind.

When developed, concentration is the meditative quality that *results* in ease in mind and body, thus providing us the composure for the two forms of meditative development. Skillful one-pointed concentration is what supports us to *identify* dukkha clearly, the first of the two investigative practices. We need to be able to stay focused on difficult or charged

---

* While I have, in this section, touched on the window of tolerance as a way to acknowledge that white supremacy culture and other oppressive systems can produce trauma, by no means is this section exhaustive, nor is it a substitute for professional support for thorough trauma healing work. Please seek such support when needed.

experiences to be able to see them clearly as reactions from the past that were taught to us about how we should or shouldn't behave.

Skillful Concentration can also increase our capacity to *be with* dukkha, the second aim of the practice instructions of the First Noble Truth. The deep settledness that is the result of the stillness of a concentrated mind supports us to be able to "sit" with dukkha and to identify clearly with groundedness what's going on. In this way, we can increase our capacity to be with our own suffering. When we're able to do so, our capacity to be with others' pain and suffering also increases, and thus our capacity to access compassion to the suffering of the world also increases.

Basic one-pointed concentration is paying attention to a specific object of practice. It's focusing, or refocusing over and over again, on a sensation, emotion, or quality of thought you want to investigate exclusively. As such, I often frame it as an awareness that excludes. You have to exclude in order to be able to concentrate well. For instance, when you begin your meditation practice, you choose one point to focus on, your meditation object—be it breath, sitting bones, or the aim of the practice you're trying to do here and now. Then, to help build concentration, you might need to get up to close the door to keep out the noises from other rooms. Or, you're distracted by the noise outside your window, but you make diligent mental effort to stay focused on your meditation object. These are ways of excluding distraction to stay with your point, or object, of focus.

When we're able to repeatedly *exclude* distractions while applying direct and sustained attention, or focus, the *result* is that the mind will be able to achieve a settled, composed stillness, increasing our ability to *discern clearly and fully* the subtleties of what's happening right here and now. Thus, concentration is a practice that can support our ability to investigate clearly and fully what an experience of racial trauma entails, such as where we feel it in the body and how it impacts the rest of our lives and relationships. As we've begun to understand trauma and its effects more, we realize that it's a whole-body experience, and thus, to heal from it is whole-body work.

Most of us tend to focus on the narrative, or story, about past racial trauma. However, trauma is very much experienced by our whole system.

People often come to meditation practice wanting their minds to become "calm and quiet." The paradox is that it's bodily ease that best supports being able to be with our experiences (present or past) so that new or clarifying insight can be achieved. Again, in the teachings, the felt-sense *results* of Skillful Concentration are talked about as deep, body ease. The insight about the machination of othering that I had in the zendo was not separate from the moment of deep, settled body experience. The years of mindful monastic practices and the developed concentration of the middle of an intensive sesshin gave me the body grounding to have the mind clearly know and understand what was happening without the activations of old emotional reactions.

In the Soto Zen and American Insight traditions I've practiced, we start with concentration on posture and then breath. Both are aspects of our bodies that are not dependent on any other conditions. Wherever you are, or whatever period of life you're in, both of these are with you. I always tell my meditation students that the body itself (versus our thoughts about it) is always present. There's no need to look for calm, settledness, or ease somewhere else. It's already present when we can stay focused on what's going on in the body.

RESPONSE AND AGENCY

The dukkha that we can't escape in life are sickness, old age, and death. We're practicing to know which parts of our experience of suffering we *can* alleviate or end.

When dealing with systemic issues like racism, it can often be difficult to discern where we have agency in the midst of so much that is outside our immediate control. For instance, the stereotype of Asian-heritage people as perpetual foreigners in the United States is tenacious and enduring. In the past, when continuously asked, "No, no, where are you really from?" even though I'd already answered, my immediate reaction would be to get angry at the person. Now, when this happens, I don't take offense, as I realize such incidents are about the person's ignorance and not really about whether I'm a citizen of the United States or not. In such instances, when we're in the midst of actively being negated in white supremacy culture, we need to be able to respond with confidence in our experience and to attend to our pain and suffering. Acknowledging and reclaiming the worthiness of our humanity is part of the work of antiracism and where we find agency.

All of us, no matter our prescribed location in the system of white supremacy culture, need to understand and be accountable to impact, which we can think of as karmic consequences or habitual tendencies of old conditioning. To change our karma, we need to engage in reflexive practice to be able to understand that our response needs to be in context. However, knowing we can be part of determining impact isn't the end goal. Our practice is also to do our best to not create and perpetuate hurt and harm. This is not about learning to control life—your own or another's. It's about doing the best that you can to appropriately respond, and building the capacity to keep staying present so you can appropriately respond in each succession of moments.

We start out by asking ourselves, how have we learned to react to hurt or harm? Then, we need to investigate our learned habitual reactions so that we can make skillful choices in how we respond. If we don't, we're more likely to go on autopilot, following our learned reactions.

It is neither necessary nor helpful to judge ourselves in how we were conditioned to react. We all have habitual energy and not all habitual energy is bad. For instance, brushing your teeth every night before you go to bed is good habitual energy to continue, and it's certainly learned. I never brushed my teeth as a young child in Vietnam before I was adopted. Luckily I had really good teeth then because I didn't eat much sugar!

So much of Buddhist practice is about being able to learn to see our unconscious habitual conditioning *and* then to be able to not be propelled by it. We can know that we have agency, or choice, and recognize unskillful ways of thinking, speaking, and behaving, and then divert or stop ourselves from those behaviors. Skillful Concentration gives me settledness in the midst of the wobbliness of conditions—whether they are my emotions, my thoughts, my reactions, or the world's conditions. It gives me a sense of balance, a stable base from which I can be intentional with my next thought, emotion, and action. This is agency.

There's a koan in which a Zen master is asked, "What is the teaching of the Buddha's entire lifetime?" The master answered, "An appropriate response." Of course, most of us wish that there was one "appropriate response" we could use as a cookie cutter for all our experiences. But the koan means that we need to find an appropriate response *in each encounter*. The appropriate response is the one I'm willing to engage with and stay for the consequences. We do our best to make wise, skillful choices, but we can't know the results. The results arise simultaneously with the interaction. Practicing like this, we become more aware of consequences, seeing and using each instance as an opportunity to shift habitual karmic tendencies.

Pausing is key to finding appropriate agency. As we continue our practice of Skillful Concentration, the quality of clearly observing and being settled with dukkha deepens, and there can be a "space" between our strong emotions and thoughts. This is a quality that's embedded when I describe "settledness" or "groundedness." Concentration and mindfulness strengthen so that we can observe thinking and its corresponding actions better, increasing our ability to make wise, skillful, and empowered responses that reflect what's important to us now.

Thinking back to the zendo and that fateful moment in the practice period, one of the many harms was that there was separation from the sense of wholeness. With those words of commentary, that teacher voiced a set of entitled assumptions that created othering. This is the most fundamental harm of racism: a disruption from wholeness and of all of us together, belonging. We start from wholeness—that we're part of the Net of Indra, of Life. To heal from racial trauma, we need to be able to reconnect to this wholeness even though others may still be traveling on old racist and entitled strands of the net.

To practice Skillful Concentration is to develop the ability to access *and* establish a steadiness to live in harmony, to cocreate the net of interconnectedness, and not just as a wish or ideology. In our everyday life, we have to be *committed* to investigate how and when we do, or do not, enact this interconnectedness. We can reenact harm or create new hurt and harm if we don't pause before we react from our learned habitual conditioning, disrupting the wholeness that is life itself.

By refocusing again and again, we gain the capacity to stay. And then with repeated practice we're able to interrupt these "drives," these learned habitual "instructions," so that we can set the course for ourselves. To go where we wisely choose to go. To be with others from, and in, more authentic and self-motivating ways.

To freely be.

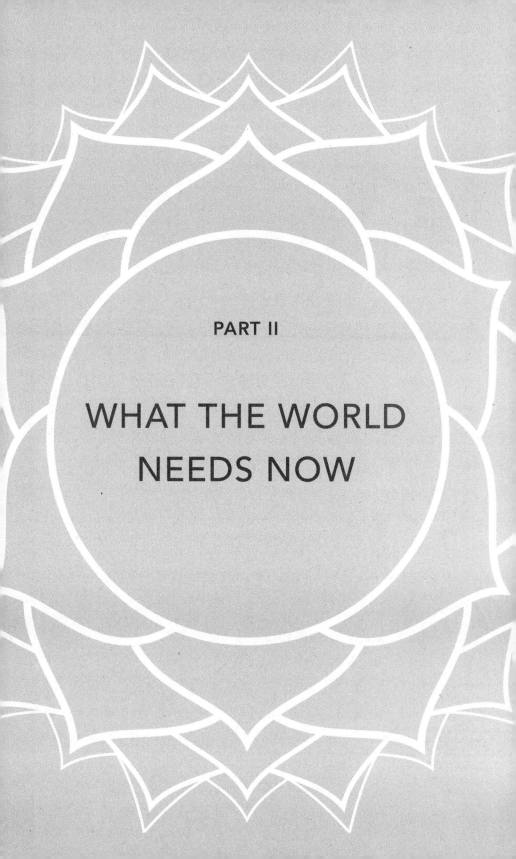

PART II

WHAT THE WORLD
NEEDS NOW

SKILLFUL MOTIVATION
Reconditioning the Field
of Awareness to Wholeness

I WAS ON A seven-day North American Insight-style retreat. There was complete silence except for two fifteen-minute interviews with a teacher in the middle of the retreat. A typical day's schedule is alternating periods of seated or walking meditation of forty-five minutes each, from early in the morning until late at night. This was also the kind of retreat where, except for during the instructions and Dharma talks, you could sit and walk whenever and wherever you wanted. Essentially, as you were not interacting with anyone directly most of the seven days, it was a great way to be with yourself completely. For an introvert, this is a heavenly experience. Whenever I'm asked in the retreat application what I want from the experience, I always say, "Silence and peace!"

On the fourth day of this particular retreat, when concentration and mindfulness had been deeply established, I went outside for walking meditation during the mid-morning. Having done many of these kinds of retreats, and quite a few at this particular center, I knew not to disperse my well-earned accumulated concentration and mindfulness by thinking too much about where to walk, so I headed to a deck area just a short distance from the main building. I was slowly walking toward a spot I had been using the past few days when, just at the periphery of my right eye, I noticed a tall white man headed for the same area. I simply pivoted left to go off to another spot, with no emotion or thought, because no feeling of ownership of the space came up (thank you, concentration!).

That's when it happened.

In my mind's eye, a light-colored wooden plaque appeared, traveling into my view from the left to the right. Carved into it in lowercase letters were the words "entitled white man." The look of the plaque was just like the one on my father's desk back in the 1970s in Thailand.

With its appearance, annoyance rose.

THINKING IS NOT PASSIVE

Thinking is part of the Wisdom grouping of the Eightfold Path and is key in this position because what and how we think determines our behavior. Buddhist teachings on Skillful Motivation (also commonly referred to as Right Intention, Right Resolve, Right Thought, or Right Thinking) lay out this progression clearly. In Pali, Skillful Motivation is *samma sankappa*. *Sankappa* literally means "thinking." However, in Buddhism, thinking is not considered to be a passive quality. It is always purposeful.

There can be a misunderstanding in the popular promotion of mindfulness practice that mindfulness is simply a passive knowing. On the contrary, thoughts gel into beliefs, which provide the drive for action. Therefore, "intention," "motivation," and "resolve" are other English translations used for *sankappa*. I will be using "motivation" because the word carries both a sense of a thought *and the drive* to act out the content of the thought.

Our practice with Skillful Motivation is to study the progression of how our thinking brings with it an embedded motivating force. As we develop our practice of observing and investigating the process of thinking, we realize that we indeed have choice and free will to choose not just what we think but also our quality of thinking. In fact, we can use our free will to direct our thinking to wholesome, useful, skillful, or positive thoughts that will drive us to behave similarly. Our thinking can bring disconnection or it can bring interconnection and wholeness. This is another reminder of why there is "Skillful" in front of each of the Eightfold Path factors. As such, the teachings of Skillful Motivation give us guidance on what kinds of thoughts are skillful and how to skillfully act from wholeness.

Since Skillful Motivation provides us a sense of knowing how we think, how our thoughts work, and how we're then motivated to act, when applied to the system of white supremacy we can clearly see how beliefs lead people to action. We have false beliefs or misunderstandings that lead us to do things that, upon more knowledge or having seen the consequences, aren't wise or skillful.

When we practice Skillful Motivation, we increase our confidence in both knowing and acting from heart and mind states that set the ground for wholeness. Additionally, we learn how we are able to restore ourselves to wholeness when delusional thinking has taken place. Agency is being able to live based on interconnection—what I call being motivated by wholeness.

"Wholeness thinking" is to let go of or renounce self-referencing, individual-centered thinking. Put it another way: to focus more on the interconnection that is the world of "we" and "us" instead of just the world of "me" and "mine." It is a renouncing of the belief that such a view or understanding of the sense of self has no consequences. We have to remember that our sense of ourselves is always *in context*. We are interconnected and always in relationship.

THE FIELD OF AWARENESS

Buddhism posits that humankind's fundamental misunderstanding is that we think that we are separate. Using the Net of Indra analogy, we focus too much on seeing just individual jewels and not enough on the net.

As we've discussed before, how the net comes to be is due to causes and conditions: how we're conditioned to seeing, building, or maintaining certain strands of the net and not others. Just as strands of the net can be repaired or strengthened if torn, we can do the same with our conditioned thinking.

Karma can be understood as intentional action (cause) and the result of that intentional action (effect), both now and in the future. Our karma, in combination with our conditioned thinking, are like a field, and the things that sprout from this soil reveal to us how we've learned to tend to our soil. In Buddhism, this is framed as a field of awareness. There are many seeds with the potential to sprout, to fully bloom and appear in the field of awareness. The ways we were taught and how we deal with the soil and its seeds are our drives, or habitual tendencies.

The beliefs we have about our own or other races, and the system of white supremacy culture and racism, are like having inherited soil. If the soil of our thought-field is depleted or has been toxified by racist thoughts and beliefs, our practice then is to recondition our field of awareness.

We have agency to affect the kind of garden we will grow. We have the ability to decide which seeds in the soil we water now, which ones we will continue to cultivate to blossom, and which ones we can shift and change. The choice is ours, individually and collectively.

It is said that the Buddha, when he looked at the way we think, saw two groups of thinking, classically called unwholesome and wholesome. The unwholesome group includes sensual desire, hatred, and cruelty or harm. The wholesome ones are the antidotes to those: renunciation, goodwill, and compassion. More specifically, when there is unskillful sensual desire, the practice is renunciation. When there's ill will, the antidote is good-will or kindness. When there is cruelty or harm, then compassion is the antidote.

I want to be very clear that desire itself is not a problem. Once again, it's about the drive or motivation behind the wanting. The translation "sensual desire" is used because it points toward how much of our lives are geared toward trying to satisfy our senses. Once at a dinner with a friend of mine who was in the import-export business, he told me that what is sold is "the sizzle, not the steak." This is a perfect example of what is meant by "sensual desire," how we are driven by our desire *for* something and not the thing itself. Marketing is all about this, creating associative qualities of wanting. Sex and sex appeal is a huge driving force in humans and so it's also included in "sensual desire."

"Covetousness" is sometimes used in the canonical teachings when talking about sensual desire. Covetousness might sound old-fashioned, but this word points toward a drive behind a desire that has the potential to bring about harmful or unskillful behavior: either as a wanting for what another has for oneself or the craving nature of desire. When such a mind-state is present in one's field of awareness around desire, then ownership and defense often become the main driving forces. "I want it for myself, and I'll do anything to have it. And once I have it, it is just for me, so I will fight to keep it."

What is "wholesome" or "useful" depends on the motivation, or drive, of the desire. Desiring to practice can be a wholesome, healthy, useful, or skillful desire. Practice can bring wholesome states of calm, especially in a chaotic environment, or as a way to augment the alleviation of critical health symptoms. However, practicing from a desire to use calmness to suppress or get rid of emotions or other unpleasant qualities we don't want in life is unwholesome because it's a form of spiritual bypass.

RENUNCIATION

When there's an unwholesome, ultimately unhealthy, not useful, or unskillful desire, the practice is to work with renunciation. "Renunciation" in the West often brings a negative connotation. However, the implication in the teachings is much more about what is gained when we relinquish. For me, "relinquish" emphasizes the *movement* of letting go versus the "what" that's being let go. Our practice is to relinquish the focus on the obsessive drive itself and not necessarily the object of desire.

The teachings talk about renouncing unskillful sensual desire in three ways. One is renunciation of the material goods of the world. The second is a group called the Eight Worldly Dharmas: gain and loss, pleasure and pain, praise and blame, and fame and disrepute. Last is the renunciation of obsessive thinking about the sense of self as only individualistic, solid, and separate.

It is said that when the "I" arises and is coveted, the other two unwholesome aspects that the Buddha saw as thinking states—ill will and hatred—arise to defend the sense of self. That is why I will focus on the renunciation of obsessive thinking about the sense of self.

Since the system of white supremacy is dependent on division based on a constructed sense of self-personification based on race and racialization, I want to talk about renunciation as a relinquishment of self. More specifically, a relinquishment of self-focus or self-referencing. We can focus more on the net itself and not so much on the jewels. Agency motivated by wholeness is to know when it's not skillful to focus on the jewel so that our connection to wholeness can be strengthened.

In Buddhism, it is taught that a sense of self-personification is embedded in qualities of thinking. To me, the sense of self-personification and solidifying around it, when applied to racism and racialization, is key. Having worked with many white people since the 1980s around antiracist work, I'm aware that for many white people, being seen as a racist person keeps them from talking about racism and its impact.

I remember hearing about an antiracist training method that involved putting a white person in the middle of a circle. Then, people would yell "Racist!" or "You're a racist!" at the person. The thought was that this method would help white people overcome their defensive reaction to their identity as "a good person" that kept them from being able to be open to hearing and appropriately responding to reports of racist incidents, especially from people of color. The assumption was that this exercise would be a way to break through what is now colloquially referred to as "white fragility." As an observer on the outside, I recall that this method was not effective.

As Asian Americans and other people of color, since we are continuously subjected to dominant ideas about our identity and those ideas typically do not reflect our lived experience, our sense of self actually needs to be built up versus broken down. White supremacy culture defines how BIPOCs "should be" in large part through stereotyping. *Stereotype,* as defined by

Merriam-Webster's dictionary, is "a standardized mental picture that is held in common by members of a group and that represents an oversimplified opinion, prejudiced attitude, or uncritical judgment."[1] For BIPOCs, we live daily with the negative and limiting impacts of these mental pictures and imputations of us that do not resonate with our own sense of being.

Therefore, part of how we can heal is to realize that the system of white supremacy is a structure based on false beliefs that limit us all. We can heal through seeing how these beliefs are constructed. As Buddhist or meditation practitioners, to clearly see how we can get caught in past thoughts and their corresponding beliefs, however valid they were before, is to be liberated from past karma and its effects. In my memory at the beginning of this chapter, I had a full understanding of how, when a thought arises along with its accompanying associative emotions and stories, it was *not* based on present conditions. Such a moment of full recognition of the process of thinking and its drive brings with it a spaciousness that choice is possible. This is freedom.

PRACTICE PAUSE

—— *Mindful Writing* ——

Who Am I Right Now?

- Think of one thing you need to do today.

- How is this task associated with a certain role or identity you take on, be it at work, home, or anywhere else?

- Now think of how accomplishing the task you need to do today reifies this role.

- Now think of something that needs your attention which takes you *away* from accomplishing today's task.

- What does this bring up? What are the emotions or thoughts that are associated?

- How many of these are related to whether, in accomplishing today's task, you'll get to "be good" at that one role?

- Does this bring more anxiety or ease?

- What happens if "being good" wasn't dependent on whether you accomplish the task right now or today?

- Is your role, your identity, completely dependent on this one task being done?

For many of us, thinking that accomplishing a task defines how "good" we are in a role drives our behavior. At times this can actually be counterproductive to our larger role. One time, when I was a social worker working with chronically unhoused seniors, a regular client came to my office. Because I had a big governmental funding report due that day, as he was coming up to the office doorway, I didn't wait for him to ask what he needed help with but just told him he needed to schedule an appointment. It turned out all he wanted was to show me appreciation for being the on-site social worker by giving me a bar of chocolate!

While it's true that a large part of my role as a social worker was to produce reports to keep this important service funded, in being overly focused on that role at that moment, I missed an opportunity to strengthen the rapport with this client. Remembering to pause so that we can choose the role *we* want to be in a specific moment, which may include renouncing or relinquishing another role, is one way to transform white supremacy's imputation of identities.

RESTORATIVE ASPECTS OF SKILLFUL MOTIVATION

We can see then that thinking isn't passive, as it brings with it other accompanying thoughts, emotions, and even sensations. As I see it, there are six restorative aspects around Skillful Motivation that can offer healing when applied to our lives.

1. Thinking as Conditioned

In Zen we often are taught that we live conceptualizing about our life instead of being in it. This means we live by our ideas about things. In my story, obviously no actual plaque was present, and so that mental vision was a vivid example of conceptualizing in action! We practice to see *how it is* that we conceptualize. Understanding thinking as conceptualizing gives us the chance to see it as what it is: conditioning.

For instance, when you read the word *apple,* what color is the apple that comes into your mind? Red? Green? Yellow? Speckled? Or maybe you thought of a variety. Fuji? Gala? Pink Lady? Some of you may even have made associations more tangential from apple as a fruit, to apple pie, apple crumble, or apple fritter. Some of you may have thought of mom, dad, or a friend, or whomever makes the best apple pie in your family. Maybe you notice desire arising with reading the word *apple* because now you want to go eat an apple.

Our consciousness makes these associations continuously. When I saw my father's plaque traveling in front of my mind's eye, obviously I was not in the 1970s nor was I a young child in my father's office. But in that instance, when I saw a man going to that walking spot, it brought about this conditioned association in my mind. And with it, annoyance arose, for two reasons. The first reason was the arising of self with ownership of the spot, so how dare he go to "my" walking spot? The second reason was how he, as a white man, would feel so entitled.

Let it be clear that a thought being conditioned doesn't make it wrong. In the system of white supremacy and the system of patriarchy, white men do have the most privilege and often feel entitled to it, consciously or unconsciously. For instance, there is the entitlement to go first at a Q&A session. My life experience has shown many instances of this and similar behavior, so it's not about whether this is generally true or not. As such, having this experience of being conditioned to associate entitled behavior with white men has validity.

Knowing *whether* a thought has validity *in the present moment* is what is most important in our practice of becoming aware of the conditioned drive behind thinking. The key then is to ask if it has validity in the current situation. Then, we can ask ourselves if we need to hold onto this thought or belief in this present interaction or in this situation. Is it skillful to keep holding on to the thought of "entitled white man" as "true" in that moment, at the beginning of my walking meditation at that retreat? No. As there were no assigned walking areas, there was no ownership of walking spots. Therefore, he was not taking a spot from me. He was not enacting entitlement or a power differential between us.

A popular Western adage asserts, "I think, therefore I am." In Buddhism, we can practice to realize that a thought can just be a thought. It's a huge moment in practice to see clearly and fully the processes of a thought coming and going, rising and falling. A thought does not have to be connected to a body-self complex. When we understand this, we can let go of associative sensations or emotions that are no longer relevant so that we can be present with this moment as it is.

When such a moment happens, it shatters the conditioning that a thought is some solid truth that you have to believe in, hold on to, act on, and identify with. With the break from the bondage of old conditioning, we can also release the hurt, pain, contractions, and harm that it brings. This allows the letting go of the identities of oneself or another that comes with conditioned constructs.

Liberation is not getting rid of thoughts. Liberation is understanding that thoughts come and go and that you have a choice over which ones are in alignment with your values now. Which ones are you going to let motivate you for how you interact with others and the world?

2. Results of Conditioning

The second way in which realizing a thought is just a thought can be healing is seeing how emotions and thoughts are often linked. In my story, I initially had no emotional reaction when I noticed another person seemingly going to the same spot to do walking meditation. This is key. My initial response was simply to pivot. I was content and at peace as I was just turning to find another walking meditation spot when that "entitled white man" thought came into my consciousness and disrupted it.

Once the thought-concept came in, *then* I became annoyed. At that moment, I habitually took on the thought-concept "entitled white man" *as a belief* of what was happening before realizing no "entitled white man" was present: just a man going to a spot to do walking meditation just like I was walking to go take a spot.

When practicing Skillful Motivation, we can more clearly see how holding on to such thoughts often further "grows" our emotions. Then we can see how when that happens, the associative *enmeshment* or tangling of the thought and the emotion are strengthened. We can see how having a thought will often bring an associative emotion.

This is why so much of basic Insight practice is trying to note the sensations of things, of phenomena. Unless you have body issues like pain or asthma, many of us live "up in our head," constantly thinking about what's going on. While thoughts are associated with our feelings, which we could call heart, there's still much more to the rest of our body that we don't pay attention to. In other words, much of practice is understanding the importance of connecting thinking somatically to posture and breath. It gives us a place to pay attention in which we don't generally have as much associative information.

3. Seeing the Process of Conditioning

When we can see the *process* of how a thought is tied to an emotion or a sensation, it can give us the space or distance to not get attached to the habitual, reactive loop of the emotion, allowing us to see it clearly for what it simply is. Just as the thought is just a thought, the emotion is just an emotion. Additionally, all these are simply passing events, and thus being aware of and following their process, versus their contents, increases our chance to heal from their old impacts.

When we can become aware and stay focused more and more on the processes of life, we strengthen our ability to simply see and be with things as they are. When we're settled enough, we get to see and hone our interest in how thinking *happens*. In the concentrated stillness on the fourth day of that retreat, I had clarity to be aware of the consequences of thinking and its drive: "Oh, this is how it arose. If I then hold on to it, that is 'belief.' In this thought, the emotion of annoyance came with it."

Such a moment of experiential understanding of the process of thinking is necessary to realize that there is choice. *The moment of seeing the process* makes it possible to realize I had agency and free will to solidify that thought into a belief and thus "take on" all the associative, enmeshed emotions and body impacts.

4. The Emptiness of Conditioning

When we can clearly see each moment of experience for simply "just" what it is, there's room with that knowing to realize the emptiness of the moment. "Emptiness" here is seeing that there was no solid and enduring "entitled," "white," "man," or "me." There was simply a series of experiences coming together out of causes and conditions. At such times we can realize the emptiness of conditions. Emptiness here means that there is no solid thought, no solid emotion, and no solid person. There is no "entitled white man." There is no "person of color getting oppressed."

In Buddhism, not-self, or *anatta* in Pali, refers to an understanding that our sense of self is not solid and enduring. When understood in this way, seeing the process shows the not-self of experience: I don't have to take on the self that *has to* have such an experience! Each experience I have is conditioned (Second Noble Truth) by the coming together of all these causes: racist and sexist history, experiences that arose when I was present and, in this case, the form (body) of this white man, the formation of thoughts ("entitled white man" as a mental view of "a plaque like on my father's desk") and an emotion (annoyance).

By this, I don't mean that we don't experience oppression. But to heal from internalized racism, we have to be able to see when oppression is *not* happening. For our restoration from oppressive forces and systems, we need to see how we were conditioned with destructive thoughts and how we've internalized them. Then we need to recognize how this conditioning can keep certain patterns of destructive beliefs and actions going.

5. Choice—Free Will—Agency

This takes us to the fifth factor of healing: knowing we have choice in what to do with such a coming together of causes and conditions.

For me, before that "thought plaque," I most likely would have gone on and on with the thought-to-emotion loop, most likely resulting in anger at the man, and then spending quite a bit of time trying to figure out what to do about my anger. I would therefore have dispersed my well-earned contentment and peace achieved through hours of concentration and mindfulness that I had worked on for days in that retreat! Most likely I would have tried to figure out "plans," which are a series of thoughts that take me out of the present moment. I would have tried to avoid him (thus, looking for him, resulting in more dispersing of concentration and mindfulness and the contentment and peace of it) or tried to find a walking place that "no one" would know about (fantasy thinking that takes me away from the well-earned concentration). And likely, my annoyance would have grown into ill will because now that man would represent all white entitled men in the world, bringing with it ill will that could have grown into hatred.

I would then have stereotyped this man, doing exactly what I don't want others to do to me. In doing so, I would have been disrupting the wholeness I was experiencing in my contentment and ease.

"Is there free will?" is a question that often comes up in discussion about karma. The answer is yes! Everything is conditioned, and therefore at this moment you have a choice about what you're going to do with what comes to you. What are you going to think and how are you going to live? How are you going to interact, knowing fully that how you do it will condition the next moment?

We don't know all the pieces that might happen. There are many conditions, so we don't always know the end result, but we can have a sense. We can be aware as Asian Americans, BIPOCs, white people, or any other racial location that hatred brings more hatred, that love will bring more love, and that wholeness will bring more wholeness.

"Selfing" is a common Buddhist term for conceiving of, sustaining, or solidifying around a sense of identity. A sense of self is going to happen. When we have a strong sense of self, what's important in practice is to investigate: Is it in service of goodwill or ill will? Does this current sense of self bring us toward compassion or toward cruelty? Being aware that our sense of self is always in context, and the implications of this, supports us to be freed from unskillful conditioned selves.

6. Wholesome Grooves

What we're doing is learning discernment about how the processes of making a self happens. When such a self arises, what beliefs does it act on? Is it toward wholeness or not, and how much of that drive to act is from white supremacy culture or other forms of oppression? And are we going to let oppression keep on motivating us toward behaviors and thoughts and beliefs that we don't want to have? I do not want to be angry all the time. I do not want to hate other people. I don't even want to be annoyed at other people, to be perfectly honest. So where is it that, when I have those thoughts and feelings, I can be aware of whether they are from the past, or whether they are useful now?

I can be aware, here and now, that I have agency to determine and act on present conditions toward a future that highlights, uplifts, and engages us all in our interconnectedness and wholeness.

GOODWILL AND COMPASSION

After working with renunciation as the first wholesome quality of thought, the Buddha offered *metta* as the second quality as the means to counteract aversion and hatred. Common translations of metta are goodwill, lovingkindness, and unconditional friendliness. To counteract harmfulness and cruelty, the third wholesome quality is compassion, or *karuna,* which is defined very specifically in Buddhism as the motivation to alleviate or end suffering—one's own and that of others. Metta and karuna are Pali words. Both of these heart-mind qualities are part of the four Brahma Viharas, or the four Divine Abodes. In Pali, *Brahma* means "supreme," "celestial," or "divine." *Vihara* means "dwelling," "abiding," or "home." Other standard translations of Brahma Viharas are "Immeasurables" or "Divine Dwellings," which the Buddha taught as easeful states.

The other two viharas, which we will discuss later in the book, are *mudita* (joy with or for others, or "inclusive joy") and *upekkha* (equanimity, also sometimes understood as balance).

PRACTICE PAUSE

Metta and Karuna Meditation

While each of the four Brahma Viharas have their own individual practices, I would like to offer metta and karuna together as they are the second and third wholesome qualities of Skillful Motivation. I'll delineate which phrases typically go with which vihara below.

The progression of the Brahma Viharas is a way for us to practice expanding the sense of wholeness—from self to close friend or benefactor, then to a neutral person, a challenging person, and then to all beings. This is a set of practices that asks you to know wholeness for yourself and then to send it out to others in increments that open you up to a larger and larger sense of wholeness. When the Brahma Viharas are used as cultivation practices, strengthening your confidence in their qualities and your sincerity as you offer them to the other categories is key. Thus, it's important to make sure you're fully at ease so you can move your body or change your visualization at any time. Additionally, you can tweak the phrases to reflect your sincere intentions.

- Begin by finding an easeful position in the body. For some, lying down or putting their hand on their heart supports this.

- First, visualize yourself in any way that can receive these phrases.
- Silently repeat the following phrases to yourself, or any variation that resonates with you:

Metta:

- May I be filled with kindness.
- Let me connect with a sense of wellness whenever I need it.
- May peace and ease be accessible to me here and now.
- May I be happy.

Karuna:

- May I connect to safety and strength whenever it's needed. (Can be a metta phrase also.)
- Let me be able to bring mercy and tenderness to my pains and sorrows.
- May I be able to forgive myself for past mistakes.
- Let me be patient with myself and with others.
- May I be free from suffering and the causes of suffering.

Nontraditional:

- Let me know that these qualities are shared by all as a connection to the wholeness of our interconnected life.

- On your next inhale, let yourself *connect to* (remember) any one or more of these phrases and qualities; let them absorb into you.
- On the exhale, let yourself *feel* their impact. Have your shoulders gone down? Is there a sense of ease in breathing or just being with yourself or things as they are?

What is wholeness in me? How do I know wholeness? By practicing in this way, we learn to develop our confidence in these qualities of wholeness. We experience a strengthening of our belief that they're true and possible; when we know this, we're more upright with these qualities. We experience firsthand that these qualities are in us. When we develop our confidence in having these qualities, our confidence grows, knowing that they really are qualities that others can also access and develop in themselves.

- Once you feel settled with these kind and compassionate qualities toward yourself, the next part of the meditation is to extend any or all of these phrases to others. One by one, offer the phrases to the following categories: close friend or benefactor, neutral person, challenging person, and then all beings.

- On an inhale, first feel the qualities in you before you offer it to the person of that category with the exhale. (For some, "radiating" the quality out to a category may feel more genuine if "offering" feels off in any way.)

- Remember, if at any time there's tension in the body, or if a phrase doesn't feel fully sincere, relax your body, or just tweak the phrase or visualization.

- Always try to end with *feeling the results* of your practice, especially in your body, as settledness or as presence.

I encourage you to memorize the phrases as they are or in your own words. Focusing on three or four phrases at a time can make this more manageable. When they come easily to you, the focus can be on connecting with their qualities and not about remembering or saying the phrases correctly.

In Buddhism, practicing to connect to and offer the Brahma Viharas is not just a matter of doing "affirmation" phrases. This is a practice of sowing seeds in our field of awareness or as new grooves in our motivations, strengthening the present and future trajectory of our thinking to positive and skillful qualities. We're also expanding our sense of these qualities to include others. Imagine if all of us knew and acted with confidence from such motivations! The net would certainly be strengthened.

○ ○ ○ ○

Identifying thoughts and their impacts on us, especially in the body, fosters healing. Letting go and the transformation that comes with it happens when we're able to be with and process our experiences skillfully. "Wholeness thinking," then, is to let go of thoughts that disrupt, deny, or lower our sense of interconnectedness and incline the mind to know and reside in wholeness.

Skillful Motivation provides us with both a way to identify how our thoughts bring with them motivation and the skillful means to do so. Let us use our thoughts skillfully toward a sense of wholeness and completeness—not only in ourselves, but with others—as a way to strengthen the net as opposed to burdening or tearing the net.

SKILLFUL EFFORT
Activating Wholeness

WHEN I FIRST MOVED to a convert monastery in California, I came with a large group of new "ongoing students," those planning to stay long term, working the center's summer resort season to earn practice credits toward the winter's intensive monastic retreat time. As the various vans unloaded us and introductions were made, a white man asked me, "Where are you from?"

"San Francisco," I replied.

"No. No. Where are you *really* from?" he persisted.

Even though I was annoyed by this typical questioning as an example of white supremacy's framing of Asian Americans as "perpetual foreigners," in an effort to be accommodating in this predominantly white new environment, I went ahead and gave him what I suspected he wanted to hear, answering, "Vietnam."

To which he responded with, "I was there in the war. I saved your people."

Once again, as it was a new place in which I knew I would be living closely with him all summer, I bit my tongue, not replying from my own Vietnamese American perspective on the role of the United States in that war.

As more summer students arrived in the next few days and similar questions of where I was "really from" continued to arise, if this vet was in the group, he would repeatedly add his claim of being a savior in Vietnam.

After a few days of this, I tried to talk with him about it, sharing how, for many Vietnamese and Vietnamese Americans I know, the U.S. presence in Vietnam was not always wanted. Even if it was desired, his framing of U.S. soldiers' part in the civil war in Vietnam as having "saved your people" was patronizing. The United States had its own political and economic motivations and stakes in Vietnam and Southeast Asia at the time, and so it was much more layered than the myopic view he was espousing.

He refused to consider my point of view and repeatedly insisted that "America saved your people." Met with his staunch stance, I started to avoid him. A few more weeks went by before I realized how much effort it took to go out of my way to avoid him in the small valley that made up the monastery in the midst of the Ventana wilderness. That, and the tightness of anger mixed with angst that came up every time I thought about his behavior, showed me that the time and energy it took from me was more than I was willing to let continue. From then on, whenever he made his claim throughout the rest of the summer, I didn't take it on. Some people may think of this as a defeated example, but this is what many Vietnamese Americans have to do to conserve our energies.

○ ○ ○ ○

In our conditioned way of thinking, most of us think of effort as just about action. In Buddhism, Skillful Effort is included with Skillful Concentration and Skillful Mindfulness as part of the Samadhi, or Meditative grouping of the Eightfold Path. Skillful Effort, then, is much more about *how to work with our emotional and mental energy to engage with our experience,* in meditation and in life. To bring us back to the Net of Indra analogy, you can think of Skillful Effort as practicing to negotiate how we use our energy to manifest, restore, or maintain wholeness and connection: first in meditation and then in our lives.

In terms of the teachings, Skillful Effort is defined as awareness that is choiceful and purposeful so that it is in alignment with a desired motivation. In the last chapter on Skillful Motivation, we discussed how we've inherited our racial karmic "seeds" through conditioned thoughts and beliefs. Following this with how we can skillfully work with emotional and mental energies will be very useful.

I'll first present Skillful Effort's four instructions for how we can work with our energies skillfully in meditation. As there are many different kinds of meditation, take these as broad, applicable ways of working with the four instructions. Then I'll apply the four instructions to the above experience to illustrate how we can use our energy when working with white supremacy culture's impacts. Lastly, I'll address a group of challenging energies called the Five Hindrances. I'll present these Hindrances as a framework of emotional and mental energies we may have been taught as ways to react to experiences of racialization or racism. I find that being able to view my habitual responses to racialization or racist incidents *as learned reactive energies* can support nonidentification and thus offers me a higher chance of being able *to respond with intentional presence and actions.*

When these energies are viewed as taught and conditioned, it increases our ability to observe, be with, and work with a memory or incident *as a series of processes* instead of only being caught in their contents. Doing so decreases our habitual tendencies to get stuck in the turning over and over again of what happened and how we, or others, could have done things differently. Additionally, as the teachings of the Five Hindrances also present ways of working with these energies, we'll see how they can provide approaches to transform unskillful karmic habitual tendencies into skillful ones.

THE FOUR INSTRUCTIONS OF PACE

Most often the four instructions for Skillful Effort are presented as prevent, overcome, cultivate, and maintain. As these are guides for how to be skillful with your energy, being able to memorize the four is useful, so I'm offering them a bit differently, as an acronym, PACE: **P**revent. **A**bandon. **C**ultivate. **E**xtend.

To pace yourself is to do something in a way to avoid overexerting yourself and to sustain your stamina, so the word echoes the sense of how we can be skillful with effort. Skillful Effort's four instructions are further divided into two divisions: unskillful and skillful. Traditionally, these pairings are worded as "unwholesome and wholesome," but as those can sound judgmental, I'll be using "unskillful and skillful" and "not useful and useful." The framing of "not" is first because these instructions stress how we can be proactive to *prevent* unskillful effort. Here's how the two divisions work with the four instructions as laid out by PACE:

Practicing with effort that is **unskillful:**

Prevent it from arising.

Abandon it when it is present.

Practicing with effort that is **skillful:**

Cultivate its arising.

Extend it when it is present.

Prevent

When we go to a retreat or meditation center, we receive the rules or advice for meditation. Many of these are to prevent distractions. For instance, when I teach my meditation course to the general public, I say, "Don't do it on your bed!" It's preventative to not use it as a place for meditation because that's where we sleep. For Zen practitioners, since we are instructed to have our eyes slightly open, we face a wall because then there is less stimulus. In the Insight tradition of meditation, usually you're seated in rows, so the instruction is to close your eyes to prevent being distracted by activity around you. In both traditions, during retreats, you keep your eyes down as much as possible once off your cushion to prevent the dispersion of meditative concentration and mindfulness.

Working with our energy in meditation is key. While the Buddha did say that we can meditate while sitting, standing, walking, or lying down, the seated posture is most emphasized because it is considered the position that offers us the best balance of energy to achieve clarity of awareness: the balance between having to expend a lot of energy to stay standing up or the collapsed energy that's often the result of lying down for an extended period of time.

Balancing our energy while working with the impact of white supremacy is also crucial. While true for everyone, for people of color, this is especially so. For many of us, having to choose practice over being able to express our whole selves is a common and pervasive position we are put into within white-centered practice spaces.

Abandon

When an unskillful thought or emotion arises, how do we abandon it? We really need to be very ardent in our effort. As indicated before, the classic translated word for this is "overcome," which gives you a flavor of how hard it can be to abandon and, by extension, what degree of ardency is called for.

For instance, at the beginning of a meditation period or retreat, most of us have to make diligent efforts to not be distracted. As I tell many beginners, the first ten minutes or so of your meditation is to just stay on a posture or breath point as your meditation anchor.* It doesn't matter if there's a dog barking next door, or if you have a vision of what you think is divine, you need to abandon letting yourself get interested in that. "Paying attention to whatever is going on" can be a meditation instruction, but to achieve one-pointed concentration, what is needed is to have the ability to stay on a *chosen* object of awareness. Paying attention to anything else at this point is "unskillful" toward the establishment of concentration and thus needs to be abandoned. Usually any undirected activity in the very beginning of any meditation period, besides staying or returning to your anchor point, is still just distraction.

---

* Like the Practice Pause in chapter 2, "One-pointed Concentration Breath Meditation."

Cultivate

Whenever unskillful mental or emotional qualities are overly strong, we can turn to cultivate skillful qualities. To "cultivate" in this context is simply to direct or redirect our attention to positive or easeful qualities. Generosity and virtuous conduct are two qualities that the Buddha often put at the beginning of many lists of practices for this reason. Metta, karuna, and the other Brahma Viharas are qualities the Buddha prescribed as "antidotes" to challenging emotions. We will cover these in the Five Hindrance section later in this chapter and throughout the book.

Cultivation of easeful mental and emotional qualities during meditation offers us a chance to practice knowing, connecting with, and resting in them with intention. This strengthens our ability to access these qualities in moments of challenge or distress, such as when working with old or present experiences of racialization or racism. Additionally, the more we are able to know and access easeful qualities, the more confident we become that they are emotions and mental states *available* to us *at will,* thus empowering our sense of agency for self-regulation.

Extend

When skillfulness is present, how do you extend it? One way is to notice in your body, emotion, or mind when you are in the midst of a positive or skillful state or experience. Many of us think that to meditate is a series of "doing." Rather, the opposite is true; instead of thinking what else you're "supposed to do next" while meditating, once you've applied a meditative tool or method, just stop and be. I often tell my students to just rest as a way of extending.

In terms of antiracist work, we need to be able to rest and extend our awareness of well-being and ease as a countermeasure to the impact of hurt and harm from racism. Many of my friends who are teachers of color and I have been saying, "Rest is revolutionary!" Systems of oppression are continuously telling us we're lacking in some way and so need to strive, thus to unplug from such expectations can be a form of skillful resistance.

For instance, the Model Minority trope presents Asian Americans as having overcome white supremacy's racism because of hard work and advances in education and economics. In doing so, it created the expectation for many Asian Americans to be high achievers, making strenuous effort pushing through personal needs and challenges to progress higher and higher. The myth was also used as a way to pit other races, especially Black folks, against us with messages such as, "If they, in working hard, have 'made it,' why can't you?" and thus promoting the old American myth of individualistic "pull yourself up by your own bootstraps" as a distraction from the machination and impacts of structural racism.

If you've cultivated metta or one of the other Brahma Viharas, extending is remembering to let yourself feel their qualities, acknowledging and resting in the positive result of your practice. Extending is useful as a reminder to us that when unpleasantness or difficulty *isn't* present, that's a moment to realize that we *are* in a positive or healing moment. This supports us to remember that, even under oppressive forces, our lives are also full of ease, joy, and connections, reminding us to rest in the completeness or wholeness of our being. We need to remember that we are here to thrive, not just survive.

○ ○ ○ ○

As is true of any instruction, an example of a skillful response may fit in more than one category. Remembering consequences—thinking through an event's possible results—can be both a prevention and a cultivation practice, depending on context. Once we start to know our habit patterns of thoughts and emotions, we can realize that what usually serves as a cultivation practice may be used as a prevention practice. For instance, if you are experiencing a lot of self-judgment as you start a meditation, instead of starting with following your breath to establish concentration, you can begin with metta phrases as a way to give your mind a positive quality to counter the self-judgmental thoughts, supporting you to settle down and be grounded.

Skillful Effort is using energy that is purposeful, useful, and appropriate toward your goals. Suzuki Roshi, in a 1969 talk, explained that "the way we behave, the way we do, should always be renewed according to the time [and] according to the place you live. On each situation, we must find how to live [and] practice our way. This is right effort." Discerning what is Skillful Effort in any given situation is, in Suzuki Roshi's words, a practice that "will be continued forever."[1]

Continual practice with the four instructions connects us to energetic wholeness, activating Skillful Effort in interactions within ourselves, with each other, and with the world.

PRACTICE PAUSE
—— *Mindful Writing* ——
Restorative PACE, with an Example

Here are the steps, and then I'll give you an example:

1. Clearly state the action you want to investigate.
2. Evaluate one **unskillful** outcome from this action.
3. Reflect on a way you want to change this energy.
4. State the theme you want to address.
5. Identify the restorative, or *skillful,* motivation or quality desired.
6. Apply **PACE**.

Example: Using the memory at the beginning of the chapter:

1. **Clearly state the action:** Answering people's conscious or unconscious racist questioning of my Americanness.
2. **Evaluate one *unskillful* outcome from this action:** Using energy to give in to white supremacy culture's expectations when asked, "Where are you *really* from?"
3. **Reflect on a way you want to change this energy:** Stop using energy as a defense.
4. **State the theme you want to address:** How to best use my energy when faced with conscious or unconscious racism.

5. **Identify the restorative, or *skillful*, motivation or quality:** Conserving energy for my own well-being of being grounded in my location as an American no matter the conditions.

6. **Apply PACE.**

Practicing with effort that is unskillful: Using energy that gives in to white supremacy culture's expectations when asked, "Where are you really from?"

- **Prevent** it from arising:

- First response: avoid such people. But it's not always possible. Plus, doing so takes energy *from* me that I'd rather put toward thriving versus defending. Thus, the clarified *useful response* to practice with is *to prevent the loss of my energy as a reaction to another's racialization of me.*

- **Abandon** it when it is present:

- For me, the clarity of the useful response from Prevent led to a natural outcome to this second instruction: to abandon the conditioning to "be nice" when in the midst of white supremacy culture settings. Put another way, I have to *abandon the conditioning that my location as an Asian American means I need to put white people's comfort above my own.*

Practicing with effort that is skillful: Conserving energy for my own well-being.

- **Cultivate** its arising:

- *Cultivate reclaiming my energy* by remembering this is *the other's* conditioned ignorance of the racist implication of their question, or, such as the case of this memory, their conscious desire to perpetuate racism. Cultivate energy for my own well-being by being grounded in my location as an American no matter the conditions. Also, cultivate (versus avoid) settings in which I am affirmed, or at the very least, not the target of direct racial hatred.

- **Extend** it when it is present:

- *Remembering to rest in the reclaiming of energy toward well-being as a way to extend having engaged in a skillful effort. I* can also extend my groundedness on this by accessing antiracist settings.

While the memory used happened a while back, I've used it for this PACE example for several reasons. Obviously this is a common, typical experience of Asian Americans with the perpetual foreigner stereotype. Additionally, it had specificity to my experience as a Vietnamese American. Additionally, it is useful to apply PACE to an old experience as it inherently already has the distance of time so that there's less charge. I also chose an experience in which there is some aspect of having executed a habitual response that has a sense of not having gone as well as I would have liked.

Because the format of PACE begins with "unskillful," I find it to be especially pertinent as a restorative tool. I would typically turn away from actions I've labeled as "failed." Revisiting an old challenge with the mindfulness tool of PACE offers us a chance to clarify our *motivations* for how to meet chronic, oppressive situations with graceful agency. After applying PACE, it's likely that not all four instructions will be remembered the first time a similar incident comes up. However, just having the clarified motivation for the outcome will likely remind you of one or more of the ways to prevent, abandon, cultivate, and extend. With repeated Skillful Effort practice, your own formulation of the four instructions of PACE becomes more easily remembered, increasing your ability to redirect and transform old habitual energies.

For me, Skillful Effort's four instructions of PACE have been a life-affirming tool. It so clearly lays out a method that is inspiring and practical at the same time, supporting me to be able to assess and practice balancing my energies to be able to be fully engaged in my life, including anti-oppression work. May it be of similar support to you.

○ ○ ○ ○

WORKING WITH THE
FIVE HINDRANCES ENERGIES

The Five Hindrances are mental states that keep us from being fully present. The Pali word is *nivarana*, meaning "covering" or "that which covers."[2] The Five Hindrances are sensual desire, aversion and ill will, sloth and torpor, restlessness and anxiety, and skeptical doubt. Traditionally they are included in the Meditative grouping of the Eightfold Path and are taught as qualities that hinder the achievement of deep concentration, hence their name.

We can also see that they are qualities we can have at any time. My guess is that, at least once, while reading this book, you have had one or more of these states. Or, recalling a meeting or class you've been to, have you not had one or more of these states? They are normal states that all of us experience. The problem is that we often take them to be more than what they are—simply states of mind that come and go like all states. This is why I like to say that they are a problem when we're *careless* about them. They hinder us when we are not careful to remember them for what they are but instead take them on as solid moods or even as personalities.

As such, let's see how the Five Hindrances can be states that keep us from being able to stay with racial memories or experiences, thus keeping us from being able to appropriately or skillfully work with or respond to those experiences. In particular, we will examine how the Hindrances can solidify into identities that we take on or impute onto others in hurtful or harmful ways.

Sensual Desire

This first category of the Five Hindrances is called sense desire or sensual desire. The desire itself is not a problem. In the teachings, it is said that a sense of "self" easily arises when a desire is activated through one of our senses. In Buddhism, we have six senses: seeing, hearing, tasting, smelling, touch, and mental formation. As you can see from the list, five out of six are what most of us think of as sensory. Bodily comfort is a big part of our life.

This is why we spend so much time making sure we have the right cushion or that the meditation hall is the "right" temperature. Most retreat centers I go to have rules about how no one can open or close windows or touch the thermostat unless you're the designated person to do so.

While this category of the Five Hindrances is also called "sense desire," the term *sensual desire* points directly at how, when we engage with our senses in an obsessive way, *that* is when they become a hindrance. For instance, let's say you smell french fries while you're meditating. Smelling is a sensory experience. However, you start thinking on and on about how you're going to eat french fries after the meditation period, and not just any french fries but the ones from the restaurant across town, and find yourself planning for ways to go get some, what route you'd take, or whom you'd go with. Now you have gone into sensual desire in a way that has hindered you from establishing concentration in that meditation period.

As applied to a sense of self, this Hindrance can "cover up" an identity that we are uncomfortable with. For years, what kept me from moving during meditation most was my concern over my self-image and what I thought others would think of me if I moved: "She's not a good meditator." The irony, of course, is that most people either have their eyes closed or are too focused on their own identity fears to notice.

In the realm of race, we can see this as an idealized sense of self, such as the wish to not seem like "a racist person" as that is commonly deemed as being "bad." Racism's hold over many of us occurs both in imputation of identity and, with that, often an assigned character judgment. For instance, in the past several years, it has become clear that "white fragility," or the state in which even a minimum amount of racial stress becomes intolerable for a white person as they are afraid of being seen as "racist," triggers a range of defensive moves.[3] Because of this, it keeps white-identified people from not only seeing their part in racism but also limits them from interactions with BIPOCs and to being with their own humanity.

To illustrate its characteristics, each of the Five Hindrances have a water analogy to go with them. Sensual desire is compared to dye in water—the dye colors the water, making it hard to see clearly. Like dye in water, idealization or concretized identity colors our perception. Racialization is based on stereotyping what kinds of identity each race "should" be. This is why so much of our work is to notice when we have taken on and solidified self-identities or when we're imputing concretized identities onto others. Either way, we limit ourselves and each other. So we practice *abandoning* such unskillful thinking or beliefs, applying the *a* in PACE.

I know someone who went through a six-month Buddhist training to work with white privilege and entitlement. They learned that saying, "I'm an ally," isn't useful because it implies that you're "done" with race work, like you've reached a goal and so can say, "I'm not a racist; I'm an ally." It's not an identity or a place to reach. Instead, saying, "I'm *acting* as an ally," with the emphasis on the verb, reflects that it's an ongoing process and that one keeps reengaging with it. Mistakes will be made in antiracist work, and so being open to keep on engaging is the key. This is a practice of *cultivating* skillfulness for what has not yet arisen, applying the *c* in PACE.

Aversion and Ill Will

With identification, or selfing, blaming and shaming often also co-arise. The second Hindrance is aversion and ill will, known as hatred in some lists. The energy in the water metaphor is that of boiling.

I used to live where there was a hot spring. It was lovely to feel its heat, but if you got too close to the water's source, you could get burned. Or, if you stayed in the hot water too long, you would get heat exhaustion. This again points us toward how if we're careless with the Hindrances, then harm can happen. The arising of feelings and thoughts of harm is something humans do. *What* we do with it is the key. Seeing clearly through strong, difficult states provides us the pause and agency to act in nonharming ways.

Aversion, ill will, and hatred are pretty obvious as part of white supremacy culture and racism. But what about righteousness? As an activist and a "fighter for social justice," I have had a lot of righteous anger. My root teacher, Zenkei Blanche Hartman, tells a story in her book *Seeds for a Boundless Life* about a life-changing moment when she was able to recognize her righteous anger. She was an activist all her life, so participating in marches and rallies was very common for her. During an anti-Vietnam War rally, she found herself face-to-face with a riot cop and recognized a way to understand their shared humanity.

> [T]he policeman was trying to protect what he thought was right and good from all of the other people who were trying to destroy it—and I was doing the same thing. Since I had no basis for understanding the experience of shared identity with someone whom I had considered completely "other"... I began to search for someone who would understand it. . . . That's how I came to be an ordained monastic.[4]

What qualities do we want our antiracist work to have? Hatred? In righteousness there can be a lot of blaming and shaming. The movement of aversion is to push away. Certainly our healing from racism and antiracist work is about pointing out or acting in ways to move toward or resolve something or someone being harmful, but we can do it in ways that do not perpetuate hatred. What is the energy that is in service of us not othering others just because they other us? Are we going to do that to them? Can there be a sense of conviction that doesn't include aversion, ill will, and hatred? Instead, can it be from unconditional friendliness? Are we behaving or speaking in ways that are inclusive? The practice to overcome aversion and ill will is to cultivate connection.

PRACTICE PAUSE

Mindful Reflection on Defusing Othering

- Imagine yourself across from someone whom you are having difficulties with. Choose an easy "difficulty," as this is an exercise to build skillfulness, not to "get through" anything or to "fix" yourself or the other person.

- Now, turn your attention inward.

- What is a mildly strong emotion you're experiencing when you think of this?

- Now bring your attention to a body location.

- What's one sensation you're experiencing that's difficult to be with?

- How can you attend to that sensation to ease it?

- Let yourself do it. Maybe a deep breath, dropping the shoulders, or opening a fist?

- Now imagine really looking at that person.

- Imagine they are doing the same exercise. What might they discover?

- What might be similarities in both your experiences?

As stated in chapter 4, "Skillful Motivation," metta is often emphasized as the practice to work with ill will. One of the translations of metta into English is "unconditional friendliness." For me, to be willing to see the commonality of our experiences even though we don't agree (even in passionate ways) is the epitome of practicing "unconditional friendliness."*

Sloth and Torpor

Now, if the water metaphor for the Five Hindrances is a body of water, sloth and torpor is the section of the pond in which algae and water plants grow so thick that it's hard to see the water itself. Sloth is heaviness and torpor is dull mental qualities.

When I'm at the Russian River in Northern California, I kayak most days. Due to the climate crisis, California has experienced extreme drought the past few years. With each year, the river water levels have gone down lower and lower. At a certain point, the algae and water plants bloom and become very dense, a thick carpet of green slime, making it hard to paddle

---

* See the "Metta and Karuna Meditation" Practice Pause in chapter 4.

through. It takes a lot of effort, my arms straining with each stroke. At the same time, the algae and water plants are luscious, bright green.

When my arms are too sore with the effort and I stop paddling, the kayak comes to a dead stop with not even the slightest advancement from the last stroke. The immediate stillness feels settling. The complete motionlessness feels very attractive. It feels so easy to just give in, to stay right there and never do anything ever again. It's hard to think about anything else except to give in to this thickness of inactivity. This is sloth and torpor. It is a state where I am pulled into the sense that it's a letting go, imagining it's a kind of nirvana, where I'm suspended and don't have to make any more effort. It is enticing, but if having the energy to have clarity of awareness is our aim, then it's a false settledness.

In terms of racial dynamics, sloth and torpor can manifest as tiredness from having to struggle to just survive in the midst of intense racist conditions. However, like all the Hindrances, the condition itself isn't the issue. We want to find out what the sloth and torpor are covering up. Sometimes during a retreat we might want to take a nap to see if it's simply body tiredness. However, if you find that doing so doesn't give you energy after, then it's time to investigate (the practice instruction of the First Noble Truth) to see if it's the result of feeling discouraged or the lethargy of defeatedness.

This is a hindrance of low to no energy. It's the kind of energy state of having given up to go down with the sinking ship. You feel like abandoning yourself into the lull, to be pulled into a collapsing of energy that seems so restful. Especially when our experience of racism is an onslaught day after day, giving up can be enticing as a means of escape. As such, it can be a form of disassociation or disengaging from what's happening.

This can feel good in the moment, but it's not what skillful practice is about. Without energy to practice, especially as a means to investigate, we stay ignorant. Skillful Effort supports clearly perceiving the conditions around us. What can support us to stay connected or feel energetic in our lives? How can we add energy?

At first, it may be upping your effort to resist the pull of sloth and torpor, to resist an internal or structural pull to just keep things as they are. Sloth and torpor may be a form of resistance to what is, a way of running from being with it. That's why it's important to be able to clearly identify what is off-kilter or needs to be worked with. Being able to name what is disrupted or torn is a way to overcome the lull of being stuck in an unhealthy status quo.

Engagement and cultivating curiosity are great ways to bring in energy. In activist work, when you're feeling stuck or discouraged, this means becoming curious about different ways or a different kind of energy you can use to engage with where you feel stuck. For example, if you're feeling isolated or alone, getting together with people with similar values or aims toward that issue can be a way to add energy. It could be for a specific action or just for a friendly gathering as a means of connection for uplift. Joining rallies, marches, protests, or organizations that are doing meaningful work can give you a sense of communal empowerment.

Restlessness and Anxiety

At the other end of the pond, restlessness and anxiety are compared to the choppy water kicked up by strong winds, making it hard to see clearly the water's surface or what's underneath. The opposite of sloth and torpor, this is the Hindrance of having too much energy. You're so agitated you can't sit still or think clearly. The practice instruction for restlessness and anxiety is concentration, to keep on refocusing on what is here, what is present, and what you *do* know instead of focusing on imagined threats or fears.

It is true that lack of safety can be a very real issue. For Asian Americans, anti-Asian hatred has impacted us particularly in recent years. A Pew survey conducted in April 2022 reports 63 percent of Asian American adults say "violence against Asian Americans in the U.S. is increasing" and "about one in five . . . worry daily (7 percent) or almost daily (14 percent) that they might be threatened or attacked because of their race or ethnicity . . . ." For those who responded that they "worry rarely or more often, about a third of Asian adults (36 percent) say they have altered their daily schedule or routine in the past twelve months due to [these] worries . . . ."[5]

Restlessness and anxiety about our safety is completely understandable as a response to fear. This is not a way of invalidating our fears. The key is to bring awareness as to whether this fear for safety is a *current* need. It can be useful to take a moment to investigate and ask yourself some questions about your fears, to ground into both your own presence and the present.

PRACTICE PAUSE
Mindful Writing

Investigation of Fear

Settle into yourself by taking a few deep breaths. Then ask yourself these questions, one by one, taking a deep breath before writing your answers. Let yourself say whatever needs to be said, trying not to edit as you go along:

- Identify an ongoing or recurring fear that you have, or a fear you are feeling right now.

- Does this fear or anxiety have validity *in this moment,* or is it habitual hypervigilance that's **taking my energy away** from being present with myself *now*?

  - If yes, how?

- Is it **taking me away** from the situation I'm in *now*?

  - If yes, how?

- Is it **keeping me from being connected** to those I care for and love *now*?

  - If yes, how?

Settle into the answers. Really feel them "land" in the body as a truth for you right here and right now. Feel it like a root anchoring you to the earth.

Based on the information you discovered from answering these questions, continue answering the questions below. However, before you continue, discern if now is an appropriate moment to figure out what kinds of boundaries, if any, you will need to make or adjust to attend to your level of safety. It is always okay to take care of yourself and wait for a more appropriate time.

Remember to take deep breaths before writing replies:

- Is what I'm experiencing enough for now?
- Can I, or can this, wait until later?
- Am I remembering I can say no?
- Do I feel safe to say this is not right?
- Is this an appropriate time to protect myself?
- What do I need to do to connect to safety?

Settle into the answers, letting them land in your body as a truth for you right here and right now, anchoring you to the earth.

Similar to working with sloth and torpor, concentration is also a great antidote for restlessness and anxiety. You want to be able to find the steadiness that concentration provides to support reconnection with your motivation or what's important to you. This helps us to ground ourselves. From stability, it's more likely wholeness-based options will arise for you. Perhaps you can focus your energies toward working on a topic or cause that's important to you. Being with like-minded people can be connecting, so joining groups to bond together can be helpful. However, with this Hindrance, take care to find a group that provides you grounding, producing an outlet for your excessive energy, versus one that riles it up further.

Skeptical Doubt

Connecting to steadiness also supports overcoming skeptical doubt. The hindrance of skeptical doubt is not just regular doubt. You'll know it by its obsessive, pervasive energy. It tends to be ongoing, often in circular or preoccupied thinking. The analogy is sludgy muddy water that prevents clarity. The energy is fragmented. Oftentimes when we're confused or overwhelmed, that's when skeptical doubt really kicks in. Concentration is an antidote, helping us to be steady enough to be able to acknowledge what is really here.

For instance, to be grounded enough in simply acknowledging being overwhelmed and confused can stop skeptical doubt in its tracks. Asking for help or support can be a useful response. At times, skeptical doubt covers up a fear or resistance to commitment. Investigating what's important to you can provide the grounding you need when doubt is running rampant.

○ ○ ○ ○

As you can see, many of the ways to work with the challenging states of the Hindrances involve practicing the easeful and connecting qualities of the Brahma Viharas or the meditative factors of the Eightfold Path.

We can also call on Skillful Mindfulness when we investigate and ask questions to clarify presence, goals, or values. Skillful Mindfulness offers two ways to work initially with all the Hindrances. First, whenever you sense the energy of any of the Hindrances, just stop and acknowledge it. This helps you to notice it as a *drive* and not get caught in its content. Second, notice when it's *not* present. While all Five Hindrance states are part of our conditioning, most of us will have a "favorite" one that is our most go-to conditioned reaction. Remember that the Hindrances are not a problem in and of themselves; it's when we're *careless* about their presence and believe that they *are* enduring or are personalities: our own or another's. Thus, when that Hindrance and its energy is not present, it can be a big relief, like a weight off your shoulders that you're no longer stuck to that energy or identity anymore.

The Hindrances are like energetic fields we can get pulled into. Skillful Effort's PACE provides comprehensive ways to evaluate and have the tools to unstick yourself from the Hindrances.

Often, when we have a sense of being made Other, we can have reactive fear and keep thinking, "I'm not good enough," internalizing the idea that wholeness is outside us as opposed to knowing that wholeness is right here inside us. Our practice is to return and stay connected to wholeness.

We can think of the Five Hindrances as preset destinations on a GPS system. If you have inherited someone else's car or you buy a used car, there might be presettings in the GPS to their home or wherever they went most often. Even in a new car, there's preset language based on what has been determined as the dominant language of the car's market.

In essence, we are often conditioned by all these preset directions—our habitual energetic drives for how we should react versus skillfully respond. They're like the Hindrances, these settings we've inherited, and we can't get away from them. We may be able to reset the settings, but as long as we're using any GPS or guidance system, they come with their own settings. Even if you throw out or disconnect the GPS system in the car, if you get lost and need directions, the maps or people you look to for directions come with their own "presets."

In everyday life, we have to be much more active in our commitment to investigate how we are using our emotional and mental energies. Due to a preprogrammed system, it can lead us to reenact or create new hurts and harms, disrupting the wholeness that is life. Through practicing Skillful Effort, we can work with how we are unskillful or skillful. Then, with repeated practice, we're able to interrupt these drives, these preprogrammed instructions, so that we can set the course for ourselves to go where we wisely choose to go, to be with others from a more authentic and wholeness-motivating place.

SKILLFUL MINDFULNESS
Liberation Awareness
with Restorative Reframing

I'M SEATED AT A TABLE in a bar off the university campus in Oregon. I have recently transferred here from a small college in the Midwest. How I came to attend this school was rather a fluke. My best friend at school had told me about this university, and though we both applied, I was accepted while she was not. Although we were both sad about being separated, as I had received a full-ride scholarship to attend, I decided I had to go.

I did not know anyone in this new city but had been placed in a dorm that was for transferring and exchange students, so most of us were in the same boat. As such, everyone was open and friendly, eager to meet one another. Bonds were quickly made. This was such a relief for me as I was shy, both in personality and from having been only one of three Asian Americans at my old high school of over three hundred students (the other two were my sister and the boy whose family owned the only Chinese restaurant in that town of less than 44,000 people).

Additionally, this college was known to be progressive, one of the first to protest against South African apartheid in the 1960s. When I arrived,

the school was in the midst of the current round of anti-apartheid protests, with rallies and marches, which I'd eagerly joined. Additionally, I
was taking ethnic studies classes, had joined the Asian American Student
Union on campus, and was volunteering at the city's rape crisis center.

On this day, I had been invited to join a group of people at happy hour
at a bar late on a Friday afternoon. As I sat at the table, I looked around me
and felt good—connected and settled. Next to me was a young white man.
We had just been introduced and were going through the usual getting-to-
know-you small talk. When we got to the topic of whether the university
should divest from corporations and financial institutions with holdings
in South Africa, I expressed my passion by saying, "Fuck yes, we should!"
He looked surprised, eyes opening wide, quickly scanning my face with its
long straight black hair and bangs.

He then asked, "*You* swear?"

"Damn right I do," I replied.

To be honest, I was actually as surprised as he was. Before that
moment, I had thought I was, and acted, like "a good girl." I had grown up
in my adopted family of German and English heritage with the belief that
children were to be seen, not heard, especially at the dinner table. From
the ethnic studies courses, the intersectionality training at the rape crisis
center, being part of the Asian American Student Union, and the activism
I was involved with, I had started to become aware of myself in the various social locations—of being a woman, an Asian American, a Vietnamese
American, a person of color, an immigrant, and questioning my sexual orientation—and what all these identities meant in relation to others.

After that day, I started to swear more.

○ ○ ○ ○

We have to be able to be with uncertainty, with not-knowing.

Dogen, the Japanese founder of Soto Zen, often taught that practice
and realization are not separate: In the doing is how we know and how we
realize.[1]

Our practice is a liberating practice. Which is to say we have to learn
to go beyond individual and structural. While we do live in dualities and

dichotomies, how can we also connect to the openness that's beyond duality and dichotomy?

Maybe you're saying, "Tell me! Tell me where that is! I want to get there right now." My answer is, "It isn't a place. It's right here and right now."

In Zen, we say we don't wake up to another life. We wake up to this life. We wake up to realizing how we've been perceiving or viewing things. We wake up to knowing there are other ways to be in life if we're willing to open up our view to how we perceive and conceptualize.

One way to see beyond duality is to see that it isn't *just* personal or *just* structural. They are always in relation to each other. We need to pay more attention to *how* they interact with each other. This is a way to go beyond duality.

I hope you can see that that's exactly what we've been doing as we've been traveling the Engaged Eightfold Path in wholeness. We are taught in many ways, and certainly by white supremacy culture, that the main place to enact our agency and power is as individuals. It isn't emphasized that we also have collective power. Furthermore, the key isn't asserting one or the other as "better" or as "shoulds."

A way to work with overcoming dualistic framing is to practice putting our attention and practice on how to negotiate *between* our relative and absolute experiences. "Relative" can be understood to be a personal, individualistic experience. When we hear "absolute" we might understand it as "objective." However, in Buddhism, until we are a buddha, one who *fully and consistently* perceives and acts from wholeness, we are never "objective" as we only see from our conditioned sense of the world. This is the Engaged Second Noble Truth: the causes and conditions that gave each of us our particular point of view and corresponding behavior in the world. It's not that we don't "know" absolute, it's that once we put it into words, it becomes conditioned (by language at the minimum), and thus, no longer absolute. Whenever we name absolute, it is through this body, this heart, and this mind, and thus, relative.

Essentially, while we can have a sense of a broader experience, as conditioned humans we are only able to describe and share it in relative ways. From deep practice, I realize I suffer most when I'm *clinging* to my individualistic idea, or relative sense, of what the absolute or structural "should be." Individualistic and structural are not diametrically opposed. They intertwine. They inter-are.

Understanding this can be healing. For instance, when I understood racism as a structure of white supremacy, *that's* when my healing from racism began. I began understanding that while it felt personal, it also wasn't personal because it's systemic as well. Mind you, it doesn't mean that it doesn't still hurt, but from this broader, more inclusive understanding, the hurt of the experience shifts to an understanding of its harmful impact. Paradoxically, this then gives me the "space" to attend to the hurt more as a way to let go of any lasting harm. It was a liberatory moment to realize *I have a choice* as to how much I'm willing to let a racist experience hurt me in this moment *and* from now on.

As you've received information and practice instructions from the pages of this book, you may think you have an understanding of them, and so you try them on. However, sometimes your experience doesn't feel or seem the same as what you've read. These days you'll probably do online searches or read other books, maybe even take a class or two. You gain more experience, and so for a while you think you've got it, and you know what practice is. Perhaps you've even applied it to life circumstances such as using the PACE steps from Skillful Effort. You start to use that framing during meditation: preventing and abandoning unwholesome qualities, cultivating and extending skillful qualities. Perhaps it seems to work for a while . . . and then it doesn't.

So far, you have not done anything wrong. You have been practicing the teachings perfectly. The problem is that you forget that realization, or an understanding that is deep and meaningful to you here and now, happens *as* you are doing and *as* you're practicing! Enlightenment isn't located in some momentary idea of the "absolute," nor is it in the "relative." Enlightenment is knowing when you're perceiving from each of these and when you are stuck in either of them. Being stuck (in Zen-speak, "solidifying") is the moment in which suffering has a high chance of arising. Thus, our ideas and concepts about each other and about life limit us when we're fixed in dogma and not open to possibilities.

If we want a world that's different—one that's full of trust and justice—then it has to be cocreated. Liberation is cocreated. If we want all beings to have equal say, then we also have to be with uncertainty, with not knowing. Only then can we truly listen. A liberatory world has to include being open to what we don't already know. For us to create a new world together, we all have to be able to let in something new. This is our practice: how do we investigate interactions between self and other, between self and the world?

It's true that there needs to be more emphasis in responding to structural racism with policies and other systemic means because it can't just be about you and me relating. As a person of color, I get so tired when antiracist work just stays at the personal or the interpersonal. At the same time, who is it that makes policies? People make policies. It's also people who enact policies. We can come up with policies all we want, but until we are enacting them—being accountable for them, and being accountable to one another—then they are just empty policies. To make policies that create change, we need to be open to possibilities, and that starts at the personal level.

Remember the Net of Indra? How, instead of focusing our attention on the jewels, we want to focus on the strands? What is the condition of the net that we've inherited? Some strands might be neat and straight; others are twisted and tangled. From here, we can go forth and interact with others in the world, bringing liberatory awareness of openness and possibility. To recreate this world, we will need to be open to newness, to uncertainty. This is the path of liberation.

○ ○ ○ ○

Skillful Mindfulness is part of the Samadhi, or meditative grouping of the Eightfold Path. There are two ways to understand Skillful Mindfulness: as a quality and as a practice. First, the quality is one that is both inclusive of various aspects without being overwhelmed by them *and* it's an awareness that manages and attends to anything going on that may need attention. More succinctly, I define the *quality* of mindfulness as a sense of being inclusive, embracing, and attending. Second, the *practice* of mindfulness comes from its Pali root meaning "to remember" or "to recollect." For example, when you are being "mindful of the gap" as you step from the platform into a subway car, then you're engaging in the practice of mindfulness. It is recollecting that you need to remember to bring awareness to what or how you're thinking, feeling, and doing: your body-mind complex.

THE PARTNERSHIP OF SKILLFUL MINDFULNESS AND SKILLFUL CONCENTRATION

Concentration and mindfulness work together. What makes both mindfulness and concentration "skillful" is that they are grounded in the fundamental understanding of practice (such as the wholeness of experience framed by the Engaged Four Noble Truths) and are put into action with qualities that are embedded in wholeness (such as the Engaged Eightfold Path).

Skillful Concentration is awareness that's unified through repeated focusing of awareness. As we've discussed before, one-pointed concentration excludes distraction and is directed and repeatedly dedicated attention. In meditation, this is when we choose an anchor, like a breath point or posture point, to keep coming back to. Doing so *results* in stability, which supports capacity building. In my antiracist courses, we begin with concentration practice to make sure we can establish composed settledness so that we can work with difficult experiences such as memories of racialization and racism's impacts. The stability supports the reinvestigation of old wounds in ways that allows for being able to meet it (capacity building) and (re)process it with new eyes to discover new contexts.

So how do Skillful Concentration and Skillful Mindfulness work together? One way to talk about Skillful Concentration is that it is like the eye exam machine at the optometrist's office. You put your eyes up to a machine to start evaluating the clarity of your seeing and how it may need adjustment. The machine is like concentration because it combines various lenses to provide you with a unifying view. The doctor tells you to look at a line of letters on a wall to read, then slides in different lenses in an effort to find out which is the corrective lens for your sight now. They start with your most current prescription and then they add to it.

If Skillful Concentration is the eye machine, then Skillful Mindfulness is the optometrist. The doctor has to attend to all of the various needed components of your eye exam. They have to ask you questions. They have to direct you. They have to remember insurance issues and time management to stay on schedule to see all their patients. They really need to attend to a lot of different components to make sure you are getting the care you need.

The doctor and the machine, together, provide a correct result for a prescription that gives you the chance to view the world clearly. Similarly, both Skillful Mindfulness and Skillful Concentration work together to support Skillful View, understanding wholeness.

TWO FORMS OF MINDFULNESS

In the *practice* of mindfulness, the optometrist keeps in mind the eye examination process while also attending to you. They are a technical evaluator and they are managing the doctor-client relationship. To bring in the *quality* of mindfulness, the doctor directs and evaluates accurately, but they aren't attached to what your prescription will be. They're only concerned with giving you the clearest sight in a nonjudgmental, embracing way. For instance, let's say you get flustered during the exam and have to ask: "What line did you ask me to read?" An optometrist with good chairside manner allows for confusion and kindly redirects.

Sati, the Pali word for mindfulness, is sometimes translated as "in the midst of." Skillful Mindfulness supports us to see racial conditioning clearly *even in the midst of changing and challenging conditions.* It adjusts for all the conditions, from personal to structural, and determines how we come to see and know *now.* In addition, mindfulness is always relational; there is a subject and an object in mindfulness. The lens is the Engaged Eightfold Path. The object is racial conditioning, white supremacy, and structural racism, and it is your memory or experience that's to be practiced with.

Skillful Mindfulness is also the way we're *attending to how* we practice and the quality of awareness we're practicing with, strengthening wholeness so that we can see where it is that we can alleviate or end greed, hate, and harm. Skillful Mindfulness draws our awareness to where there are patterns of reactivity and places where we can shift. At times, practice is working on our window of tolerance as we're learning to have the capacity to hold difficulties so that we don't become overwhelmed, practicing to hold such experiences with wider breadth. When our field of awareness is more flexible, it helps us to regulate our window of tolerance.

Skillful Mindfulness helps us to adjust to internal and structural conditions to support us to determine how we come to see the way we see now. The key is to realize what is truly present.

THE THREE MOVEMENTS OF CORRECTIVE TRUTHS

Another way we can practice Skillful Mindfulness is through a sequence I've developed called the Three Movements of Corrective Truths. This theory emerged from reading Cathy Park Hong's book *Minor Feelings: An Asian American Reckoning*. She writes:

> Years ago, whenever a conversation about race came up, my white students were awkwardly silent. But now, many of them are eager to listen and process the complexities of race relations and their roles in it, which gives me hope. [Linda Martín] Alcoff calls this self-examination "white double consciousness," which involves seeing "themselves through both the dominant and the nondominant lens, and recognizing the latter as a critical corrective truth."[2]

This contemporary "white double consciousness" theory is rooted in W. E. B. Dubois' "double consciousness" theory that comes through the perspective of a Black-white racial dichotomy. In *The Souls of Black Folk*, Dubois says, "One ever feels his twoness—an American, a Negro . . . two warring ideals in one dark body, whose dogged strength alone keeps it from being torn asunder."[3]

As I examined these two theories—Black "double consciousness" and "white double consciousness"—neither seemed to totally fit my experience. I could relate to how, perhaps, as a person of color, I, too, have a "double consciousness" as I have had to hold both white supremacy culture's view and my own lived experience. However, from my location as an Asian American immigrant and the in-between land of invisibility that I and other Asian Americans inhabit in the predominant Black-white dichotomy of race discussions in the United States, I started to wonder if there is a framing that would resonate better for me and people like me. Cathy Park Hong writes, "Asian-Americans have yet to truly reckon with where we stand in the capitalist, white supremacy hierarchy of this country."[4]

How can something like the "corrective truths" Alcoff writes about be put in a framework that speaks to Asian Americans' experience of white supremacy culture's minimization and dismissal of racism toward us? I came up with the Three Movements of Corrective Truths in an attempt to answer this question. And while it started as a way to reflect my own and other Asian Americans' experiences, and will be talked about as applied to race, it is a model that can be used by anyone seeking to understand and shift their perspectives on how social locations are contextual and layered. As such, these Corrective Truths are described as "movements" in mind and heart to remedy internalized oppression.

The First Movement of Corrective Truth
Assimilated Truth

The First Movement of Corrective Truth as applied to racialization and racism is seeing and acknowledging internalized or assimilated truths that have been conditioned or learned. In other words, these were unconsciously internalized as truths. In our work in this book, this has parallels to the First Engaged Noble Truth. We have to acknowledge and investigate how we were conditioned by individuals, family, religion, culture, government, or other forces to think, believe, feel, and act the way we do.

Assimilated truths are what were taught as "norms" so that you can be absorbed into a specific system's values. The way most of us have had U.S.

history taught to us has mostly been framed from a white-centered point of view that leaves out many BIPOC experiences and normalizes domination and oppressive acts toward BIPOCs as a kind of "necessity" in the creation or upkeep of this country. For example, the framing of the removal and killing of numerous Indigenous peoples in North America to promote the stealing of their land as a God-given right with the dogma of "Manifest Destiny."[5]

I do not mean that to assimilate in itself is "wrong" or "bad." In fact, for many of us people of color, we were taught assimilated truths by our family and culture to try to protect us. We had to see the white sense of things and at times to live or to work from that white-centered view as a safety or survival response. I remember how my Vietnamese mother told me to smile and be polite to the U.S. soldiers on the streets of Saigon. We were the ones who had to move out of their way if any of them were walking toward us in public spaces.

To investigate if we're operating from assimilated truth, we simply want to remember to pause to ask ourselves questions about how we were conditioned. What did I learn? What unconsciously internalized truths am I holding and operating from?

My story about swearing at the college bar was a moment of awakening to how I'd internalized the stereotypes of my social location as female ("good girl" and "seen but not heard" as most of the conversations at the dinner table growing up were about my younger brother) or when combined with being Asian ("submissive geisha" meme). These days, I'm beginning to wonder how much of my sense of myself as "a shy person" is personality and how much of it was developed from being Asian-heritage isolated after my adoption?

The Second Movement of Corrective Truth
Reactive Truth

The Second Movement is Reactive Truth. Reactive truths are often a response after becoming aware of having been assimilated or having internalized oppressive conditioning. My starting to swear more from that day on was a reactive truth. When the man at the bar showed surprise and I saw the way he looked at me in an assessing way, (and while I don't know for sure) probably not as "the nice Asian female" that is the stereotype of Asian American women, in that moment I realized I was the *epitome* of a stereotype! Then, in an effort to overcome such imputation, I purposefully swore more. However, it is reactive because it was still white-centered; to "reject" such a view is to deem it a valid "truth." The motivation for my rejection was still in relation to whiteness and the white view.

The Second Movement relates to the Second Engaged Noble Truth. It's a form of understanding the cause or origin of assimilated truth as conditioning and then actively working to unlearn and relearn. Racism, like any damaging force, causes wounds. It's natural to react in ways to protect ourselves from such hurt and harm. Our practice is to notice whether it's an old wound, its impacts on us, and how we have agency to respond to it in holistic ways now. It takes time, effort, lots of trials, and active participation. You can't just think your way through "getting over" reactivity. It takes intention and clear awareness. The PACE practice from Skillful Effort is an effective tool for working with reactivity.

PRACTICE PAUSE
—— *Mindful Writing* ——
PACE-ing Reactivity

Think of a time when you did something that was out of reactivity. If this is your first time doing this exercise, please start with something low-grade and not about race.

Now, answer these two questions:

- What was *unskillful* about what I did?

- What was *skillful* about what I did?

Then, apply PACE to how you might respond in this situation:

Practicing with effort that is **unskillful:**

- Prevent it from arising by:

- When it is present, **A**bandon it by:

Practicing with effort that is **skillful:**

- **C**ultivate its arising by:

- When it is present, **E**xtend it by:

The Third Movement of Corrective Truth
Liberatory Truth

We arrive at the Third Movement, which is Liberatory or "as-it-is" Truth. This means responding while taking into account what we know as racialization, structural racism, and our reactive patterns. From there we intentionally, with clarifying awareness, know that we have agency *to respond from an informed place.* Intentional or awareness-based mind-set *allows for* "as-it-is" Truth because we don't reject that we've been assimilated or have internalized conditioning. As-it-is Truth is a mind-set in which we're able to fully take into account our reactive patterns from a settled place. This involves having been with and processing through the reverberations of the harm of the old unconscious truths' impact on our body, heart, and mind. From settledness and with clear precise knowledge (wisdom) we respond and take full responsibility for this choice we are making right here and now, with liberatory agency.

The Third Movement corresponds to the Third Engaged Noble Truth: habitual reactions that rose from old harm or harming do *not* have to continue; new, transformative choices toward nonharming and wholeness are possible. Additionally, from thinking, feeling, and living *defined* by hurt and harm, we open up to and move toward choice and agency. I move from thinking my life is a cage to realizing it's a container. Instead of living from defendedness, I'm able to live from self- and collective agency.

It can be hard to see things as-it-is, particularly seeing that I've been conditioned to limit—and have, perhaps, even participated or colluded in limiting—possibilities for myself or others. Once I see that, then I have more agency to find a different way. This is a way to open up ourselves to knowing and being confident that wholeness is present and that change is possible.

With this shift to centering wholeness, liberatory questions such as these often arise: What is there besides dukkha, hurt, and harm in life? What do I want to fill my life with? When I put down my guard, what do I want to open up to or let in more? How can I live centered in nonharming, happiness, and wholeness? It opens us up to the possibility that is beyond just hurt and harm. We recognize that we are more than our pain.

For many years I swore quite a bit, mostly as a way to shock people in an effort to reject the "nice and submissive" Asian female meme. It was also a way to express anger for having been stereotyped in this and many other ways. With time I have also seen that as long as I'm doing it from a reactive place I'm still colluding in the system of white supremacy. Now, I do swear at times, sometimes still in anger. And while at times there can still be a hint of wanting to shock when I swear, most of the time it's because I'm expressing passion about an issue. Or as a light release from knowing that just because I don't live so much by what people think of me, it doesn't take away that I am still being stereotyped and limited by a system that is not fully aware of nor values my humanity. Still, I want to actively bring awareness to when and why I swear. I want it to be intentional and mindful, in service of connection and as an expression of my wholeness.

So much of practice is reframing or reinterpreting our experience in the here and now. Practice involves taking into account myself and the situation I'm experiencing and then being inclusive of my values as well as the conditions of place and time, and then reinterpreting how past injuries or present injury doesn't have to be harmful here and now. Instead of acting from a place of invalidation, I can act toward restoration and healing. This is about reclaiming wholeness for myself, with others, or for our communities.

○ ○ ○ ○

In Theravada Buddhism, a way to describe the fruits of deep practice can be framed in three movements: disenchantment leads to dispassion, which leads to cessation, resulting in liberation. For me, practicing the Three Movements of Corrective Truths offers similar outcomes: disenchantment with assimilated truths; developing dispassion toward reactive truth with its thoughts and behaviors based on reactivity; and then, with the cessation of reactivity, we can view our experiences and behave from clarifying, as-it-is truth, experiencing the liberation of being able to respond with intentional agency.

In each moment, are you open and willing to see a truth for what it is? Can you include that not-knowing is also present? We need to have some sense that newness and possibility is liberation. Are you willing to be responsible for the truth you see? Does it bring hurt and harm, or does it bring more connection, more love, more joy for you and those in your life? Ultimately, this is what it comes down to.

Can we not have a static or fixed sense of things, but one within context? Openness and awareness of context is one way to define Skillful Mindfulness. In the context of racism, it's largely about incorporating inclusive history and activating intentional presence that will engender a nonharming future.

I'm at Russian River, sitting on the back deck, gazing out at the river on a bright morning. I can see a long, long strand of spiderweb blowing in the breeze. I see a tiny little spider on one end, gently undulating amidst a clear blue sky. Where is the beginning of the strand? I can't see where it's attached. But that spider knows.

In the spring baby spiders hatch. A new spiderling has to be willing to jump off and trust the conditions, such as wind, to take it somewhere else where it will land and start its own web. It carries with it some inherited sense of tradition, but it has to be willing to jump into the unknown and go off on its own to start its own web, its own liberated life.

This back deck has a fence with a row of spiderwebs on it. As an animal rights person, I don't clear away webs, so now there is a whole community here.

We have to have this sense of openness to know what is present, what we've inherited, and what is important to us. We also have to have awareness that there is always going to be not-knowing. Therefore, we have to have the resilience to meet conditions in which things don't go as planned and that things can fall apart, and yet we have the capacity to find centeredness, to not be overwhelmed, and to trust our experience of wholeness as ourselves, as others, and as life conditions right here and right now, as-it-is.

PRACTICE PAUSE

Equanimity/Resilience Meditation for One and All

Remember that upekkha is one of the four Brahma Viharas. It is usually translated as "equanimity." Very specifically, upekkha here means the equanimity that comes through a deep understanding of karma, or cause and effect, or action and result. As such, I have been trying out upekkha as resilience. See how this works for you:

- Begin by settling into your posture. Sitting, standing, walking, or lying down, rock your body a little bit side to side, just enough so you feel really truly settled where you are.

- Take deep breaths, as many as you need.

- Now visualize yourself in any way that can receive the following phrases.

- Say these phrases silently to yourself:

  - I am the nature of flexibility as I meet the comings and goings of my life.

  - Joys and sorrows are a natural part of my life, and I am open and able to receive.

- Let me access clarity of heart and mind to meet the conditions of my life as they are.

- May I know that resilience is of my nature all the days of my life.

- On the inhale, connect with how you know that these phrases are true and possible.

- Just let these phrases in, let yourself know them; let them permeate, fully received.

- Feel the results of these phrases on your body: perhaps as a breeze, as a ray of light, as coming through your pores; whatever works for you.

- Now, visualize all beings, not leaving anyone out, and offer them the following phrases:

  - May all beings access flexibility within the comings and goings of their lives.

  - May every one of us be able to harmonize our joys and sorrows as they come and go.

  - Let clarity of heart and mind be our guide in every situation, in service of nonharming.

  - May the realization that our strength rests in resilience be possible for every one of us, all the days of our lives.

- On the inhale, let yourself connect to how you know these qualities are true and possible.

- On the exhale, feel these truths inside, then extend them outside. And then let yourself feel them coming back to you, like resonance, back and forth, supporting us all.

In Zen we say that the question is more important than the answer. Therefore, much of our practice is to be able to ask questions—not from invalidation, but from a sense of openness. Is this what I believe? Is this worth following now in my life? Am I open to the shifts that need to happen here and now?

How can I live knowing I have choice, or agency, in interpreting or reinterpreting what I believe, say, or do from this moment on? It starts with knowing both my location in systems and how I am on this Engaged Path of wholeness.

Individual healing and collective restoration from the impacts of white supremacy culture is challenging, demanding, and, at times, excruciating work. It takes dedication and patience. Grounded in Skillful Mindfulness, with its open, inclusive quality and its attending, managing practice energy, I've offered us the Three Movements of Corrective Truths as tools to work through and make new liberatory meanings to our suffering and the suffering of our people. To heal and restore, we need to be able to move from just surviving to thriving.

Liberatory agency supports me to know what I've gone through. It doesn't deny my experience or the historical impact of racism or other harm and harming in the world, nor does it deny that there have been missteps, misunderstandings, and misperceptions in believing in ideals or structures. And it also asserts that these beliefs don't have to be true for me, for us, or for our communities anymore. It allows us to let go of the past to be open to what the world needs now.

SKILLFUL SPEECH
Shifting Speech to Wholeness

I AM IN A PRACTICE PERIOD, a ninety-day meditation retreat, at the convert Soto Zen monastery where I've been living for three years. I am part of the *doanryo,* a selected group of senior practitioners who are in charge of organizing all the activities in the zendo, or meditation hall. This position involves tasks such as letting people know when to come to meditate and how to participate in ceremonies, leading chants, and leading the serving teams during *oryoki,* Zen formal eating in the zendo.

A white male teacher is leading this practice period. As is part of the format of any Soto Zen intensive session, each practitioner goes to see the leader of the intensive for a formal dokusan, the Zen word for a one-on-one interview about your practice, with the Abbot of a temple. Meeting with the leader one time is mandatory, after which it is up to the discretion of the student or teacher to decide if more meetings are needed. The format for a dokusan I had been trained in thus far was to bring in a question to the teacher that was about a teaching point, one's practice, or how practice can support a life difficulty. On this occasion, being the first meeting with this person I didn't know, I didn't have a question for him, so I asked him if he had one for me. He did.

"I've been watching you. You go around looking glum a lot. What's going on?"

I answered, "I am having a lot of body issues. Some of it is overwork as head gardener the past two and a half years, but most of it is that I'm having a hard time with the racism that's happening here at the monastery."

He answered, "You need to not think about yourself so much. You should focus on taking care of others."

I looked at him, baffled. I had just started to share a pain that was a result of the impact of systemic oppression, and without having had any discussion with me, this is what he had as advice?

I paused, then said, "You don't even know me. How can you say that? As an Asian American woman, my whole life *is* thinking about other people. I've been taught to always put other people's needs first. And what does that have to do with my experiences of racism here anyway?"

"Your practice as a *doan* is to take care of the sangha, a community of practitioners. So you should be putting the sangha's needs first," he asserted.

As he had completely ignored my point twice now, the subject of racism and its impact on me and thus my practice, I realized this was going to go nowhere, so I politely bowed out of the room.

○ ○ ○ ○

On one level, the Abbot was correct. As a doan, my role was to focus on making sure members in the practice period were taken care of around the *forms,* a Zen word for appropriate conduct, in the various ceremonies and skills that are part of Soto Zen practice. However, he did not act in context. His focus was limited to being an authority, and thus, commanding.

It is true that the Abbot, as the leader of the practice period, was technically everyone's boss. However, if you have a boss with whom the only interactions are about how you should do your job, how good a relationship would you have with that boss? This wasn't simply about professionalism and job responsibilities. I was trying to share how racism was impacting my ability to practice, which, I would argue, also had a profound effect on how well I could do my job. Because he was in a position of authority and he believed the job I had to do was what was most important, he did not listen to me and what I was trying to share. To the Abbot, racism was irrelevant to my practice, and he only focused on how he thought my glumness affected my ability to do my job well.

In the system of racism, white people's point of view is centered. BIPOC voices and points of view are considered less-than: from unimportant at the minimum to irrelevant. Also, to me, there was an intersectionality of oppressions in this situation. I doubt he would have pointed out to a male person that they looked glum. The predominant stereotype of Asian and Asian American women is that we should always be smilingly accommodating. Additionally, he did not know me, only what he interpreted by "watching me." We had never interacted until that moment. If he had been my teacher or was a person I had a relationship with, the result would likely have been different. The Abbot, on several levels, ignored the context of the situation, focusing only on his authority and what he deemed important.

The priority in his style of communication was not about connection or context. To live from liberatory agency in wholeness, we need to shift not just our perspective but also the ways we interact with each other and the world. Let's explore skillful means to do so as we enter into the next grouping of the Engaged Eightfold Path factors.

COMPASSIONATE CONNECTION

Skillful Speech begins the part of the Eightfold Path grouping classically known as Ethical Conduct, followed by Skillful Enactment and Skillful Living (or Right Action and Right Livelihood, classically). Since this section is about how we can relate to ourselves, with each other, and the world, I prefer the term Compassionate Connection rather than Ethical Conduct. I'm calling it Compassionate Connection to emphasize the relational quality of this section of the Eightfold Path as it directs us to manifest the Wisdom grouping of the Path, namely Skillful View and Skillful Motivation.

Within this grouping, Skillful Speech is the first factor that asks us to put into action Skillful Motivation's framing of how the drive, or motivation, of our thinking can be used. Will our speech be driven by oppressive power with its embedded division and disconnection, or toward wholeness and connection? In the Engaged Four Noble Truths framing, Skillful Speech is about shifting our motivation for speech: from simply authoritarian information giving to connection in context.

The classic framing of Skillful Speech has four elements: abstaining from lying, abstaining from speech that divides, abstaining from harsh or abusive speech, and abstaining from idle chatter. As this list is a guide to keep close to us as we practice speaking skillfully to connect, I have come up with an acronym to help us remember it more easily: TUGS. I've also put a positive spin on it.

T is for truthful. Truthfulness is layered and in context.

U is for uplifting. Instead of speech that divides, the motivation is to bring forth the positive, especially to overcome internalized self-hatred.

G is for gentle, instead of harsh and abusive.

S is for significant, instead of idle chatter.

When we go to speak, these qualities can be like a "tug" at our sleeves to remind us to ask ourselves, "Am I speaking in a way that is truthful, uplifting, gentle, and has significance?" Now, let's go through them more in depth.

T Is for Truthful

We most often think of truth as being about facts and information. We've all heard, "Just the facts, please." But facts can be manipulated, as we well know. At times information presented can be used to mislead and to deny hurt and harm instead of acknowledging racism or other oppressions. Speech around anti-Asian violence in particular leans toward minimization or even erasure.

The March 2021 spa shootings in Atlanta took place in three spas owned by Asians. The shooter was targeting Asians and six of the eight people killed were of Asian ancestry. And yet the sheriff spokesman on the case characterized the shooter as simply having had "a bad day" to explain the shooter's actions.[1] This kind of speech is either attempting to minimize the harm that Asians experience in white supremacy culture or is a denial that white supremacy culture exists.

There are also cases where "just the facts," without being placed in context, can be harmful. Due to systems of oppression, our well-being, if not our lives, needs to be taken into account. For instance, as an Asian lesbian, sometimes it is safer to lie by omission. To this day, the simple question of "What did you do with your weekend?" can be difficult for LGBTQIA2S+ people, depending on how safe our work environment is. In the early days of coming out as a lesbian, I worked in places that didn't always feel safe because the organization's DEIA (diversity, equity, inclusivity, and accessibility) policies weren't clearly and publicly known. I would use the *he* pronoun to talk about what I did with my partner in case being queer wouldn't be accepted by my coworkers.

Now that I live in the San Francisco Bay Area, dubbed the "Gay Capital of the U.S." by *Life* magazine in 2015[2] and colloquially known as such for decades, it may seem that it's perfectly safe to be out. However, when I have visitors from out of town, and we go to Pier 39, where there are many tourists from less-tolerant parts of the United States and other places in the world, I have to be careful not to hold my partner's hand or to kiss her in public. For many of us queers, how much we can be "truthful" is dependent on whether there's a clear environment of safety or not.

Many communities of color can be slow to embrace open expressions of homosexuality. When I moved to the Bay Area in 1995, I was an organizer for an Asian lesbian and bisexual group. In 1996 we became the first lesbian contingent in the Chinese New Year parade. We were so happy to be accepted! However, for many Asian-heritage folks, the spaces in which our queer identity can be expressed and where we can feel safe to be out is layered and complex. In cities such as San Francisco, with a larger LGBTQIA2S+ scene, queer people are encouraged to be "out and proud." Yet, being open about being queer isn't always acceptable within our families and Asian-heritage communities.

While a part of this could be attributed to many Asian cultures' general reticence of public display of sexuality or intimate partner affection, some of it is simply homophobia. With this in mind, and knowing that the parade was one of the biggest events in San Francisco and therefore televised, as organizers we had to find ways for people to participate that would honor the varying degrees of being out. As it was the Year of the Rat, we had different versions of rat masks and makeup for people to use to disguise themselves if needed.

I know that to this day, many Asian-heritage queers with white partners struggle with having their partners understand this need to be fluid about being out. Part of "being truthful" about our queerness as Asians is that it is variable, complex, and in context.

As oppressed people, we have to reflect on how we may have taken on valuing white-centered dominant society's idea of what is considered "significant truth" over our own. If so, we need to work with it, shifting internalized white-centered views into ways that make sense to us in our lived experiences. Of course, we do need to be mindful. It doesn't mean we can say whatever we want at any time. Another way to put it is: How can we recenter truth to be more inclusive of our complex experiences in contemporary life and, more specifically, as oppression-liberated people?

U Is for Uplifting

The classic phrasing for this factor of Skillful Speech is refraining from "speech that divides." Since a central function of white supremacy culture is to create division and fragmentation through messages othering Asian Americans and BIPOCs, we can internalize these, resulting in self-hatred. To work with overcoming oppression, I think it is especially pertinent to focus on shifting internalized speech to our own vantage point.

A practice with Skillful Speech is to identify how we've internalized "speech that divides" and then to recenter how we *can* define ourselves. One way is to find language that self-describes versus language that has been put onto us. As part of the civil rights movement during the 1960s in the United States, Asian-heritage activists renounced the term *Oriental.* Yuji Ichioka and Emma Gee, along with other activists, first coined the term *Asian American* in 1968 when they formed the Asian American Political

Alliance (AAPA) on the University of California, Berkeley, campus.[3] Asians created for themselves a new term that wouldn't define them in relation to white people.

When I came out, part of my healing was overcoming internalized homophobia brought on by the damaging ways mainstream media and society talked about queer people. My first exposure to the term *queer* came from a game learned in childhood. A year and a half after I was adopted, my parents moved us from Thailand to the suburbs of Washington, D.C., with the stated aim "to Americanize the kids." I was nine and remember being taught by the kids in my neighborhood to play a game called "smear the queer." It was a game with a simple aim: for everyone to run after the person with the ball, tackle them down and pile on top of them, thus to "smear the queer."

Consequently, for many years I was upset when people called me "queer," though my relationship to the word started to change as the context around the word changed. I'm so grateful for having lived through the 1980s and 1990s when we took back the word *queer* with Queer Nation.[4] Reclaiming a derogatory word as a strength is a way to recenter speech from hateful and demeaning connotations to positive affirmations.

Not long ago I had an incident in which I was able to realize this strength from recentering, or shifting speech in myself. I used to live near the San Francisco LGBT Center. One day, as I was walking by the center with a visiting friend who was also a lesbian of color, a white guy was walking down the sidewalk toward us. As we approached the man, I thought to myself, "Oh, he seems really tired," so I smiled at him and said, "Hi." He didn't answer right away, but just as we passed each other, he jeered, "Fucking lesbians." Simultaneously, we both turned and replied calmly, "Yes, we are."

When I first came out, I most likely would have yelled after him with some angry defense. This time, after almost forty years of being an out lesbian and having overcome much internalized homophobia, I was able to respond calmly, settled in my identity. The attitude I had this time was, "You tried to diss us? Didn't work, dude."

Another thing that was interesting about this story was observing how my mind tried to deflect the impact of that man's hatred. When we turned to answer him, I saw that the *L* from the LGBT sign on the center was missing; maybe it had fallen off or broken. I remember I had a quick flash of thought, "Oh, he said the word *lesbian* because the *L* was missing on the sign over there." In my head I was making an excuse for him. It was like I was trying to fill in the blank for him.

Part of the machination of systems of domination is how we're taught to minimize the impacts of such incidents. Internalized oppression is complex and has many layers. A part of my thinking still went down the groove of internalized homophobia, minimizing the harm of what this man had done. However, in this case, I didn't let it "stick" and clearly saw it as a minimization and internalized homophobia. Seeing the series of processes and seeing how I had agency to stay in the wholeness of my being was a centering moment.

To know that we are not alone as we practice letting go of internalized homophobia and other oppressions is also key. I was able to respond to the hatred the way I did because I was not alone. I was with my friend. The synchronicity of our turning together as one to calmly reply to the man with "Yes, we are" was a vital restorative part of that incident for me.

There's a story in the *suttas* in which Ananda, the Buddha's attendant, having just arrived with the Buddha to a teaching site and looking out at the assembly of practitioners, said, "This is half of the holy life, lord: admirable friendship, admirable companionship, admirable camaraderie."

The Buddha replied, "Don't say that, Ananda. Don't say that. Admirable friendship, admirable companionship, admirable camaraderie are actually the whole of the holy life. When a monk has admirable people as friends, companions, and comrades, he can be expected to develop and pursue the noble eightfold path."[5]

Thus, we don't need to do this alone. It's my belief that oppressive systems seek to divide and isolate those who are the target of oppression. Being anti-oppression, then, is to know that we are not alone and are, in fact, uplifted when we come together to work to dismantle oppressions.

Part of the healing we must do is to learn to uplift ourselves, individually and as community, to counteract hatred we've internalized into ourselves, so that self-deprecating speech doesn't divide us from our wholeness.

G Is for Gentle

I began my activism in the movement against gender-based violence. It was a great means for helping me to overcome the conditioning as female and Asian to be quiet and unobtrusive. I developed an ability to push against and through these conditionings in order to lead rallies and marches such as Take Back the Night and participate in the South African anti-apartheid movement in the 1980s and 1990s. Through this, a sense of fierceness developed.

When I came to meditation practice, the emphasis on metta was difficult for me. Metta, as mentioned previously, is the Pali word most popularly translated into English as "lovingkindness," "goodwill," and "unconditional friendliness." If you recall from the "Metta and Karuna Meditation" Practice Pause in chapter 4, this practice is based on visualization of categories such as oneself, a good friend, a neutral person, difficult people, and all beings. In the meditation, one is guided to direct qualities of goodwill as well as qualities of peace and ease, well-being, safety, and happiness toward the subject of one's visualization. At first, I felt like it was too passive, and we needed to act more to address hurt and harm instead of just sending out positive qualities!

However, after many years of practice in general and metta meditation and recitation in particular, I understand that as oppressed people, the ability to strengthen our trust that goodwill and kindness is *possible* within ourselves and from others can have a huge impact on our healing. Since we are often put into the down-power position, it's hard to remember that our lives matter. Happiness is supposed to be what every American is "endowed" with, but we know that in reality that's not true. Unfortunately, because systems of domination prevent this from being guaranteed for oppressed folks, we have to connect to and develop these qualities for ourselves and with others. Metta practice can help us to know that well-being, happiness, and safety are part of our restoration.

The Buddha taught metta and the other Brahma Viharas, the Divine Abodes, as qualities of heart and mind that are easeful. The other three are karuna, mudita, and upekkha—compassion, inclusive joy, and equanimity, respectively. Metta is first on the list because, as I see it, the qualities that are embedded in the phrases of recitation can support us to reconnect to the wholeness of our human nature that we may have forgotten or that is hard to remember when we are faced with oppressive forces daily.

PRACTICE PAUSE
Metta for Self Meditation

While I shared a longer "Metta and Karuna Meditation" in chapter 4, I want to revisit a simplified version of metta practice that is focused solely on the self. As expressed previously, self-work and self-care are important to support us to thrive and not just survive. Practicing metta meditation just for yourself can be used as a tool for overcoming internalized self-hatred.

Take a moment to try it on for yourself with this guided meditation:

- First, take an easeful posture. Any position is fine. In meditating on the Brahma Viharas, bodily ease is important to foster emotional and mental ease. This is not a meditation to push through. At any point, adjust your body or even tweak a phrase I offer in any way that makes it easy to feel the possibility of the truth of the quality for you.

- Close your eyes if you would like. This may not be comfortable for some people. If dissociation is something that tends to happen for you, keeping your eyes softly open is recommended. If it becomes stronger as the meditation continues, stop doing the meditation and take deep breaths or look around the room and name three physical things out loud. Rejoin the meditation when you can or if you wish. Again, there's no need to "push through" at any point. Some people find it helps them to settle into this meditation by touching their heart-space.

- Say the following phrases silently or softly to yourself. In between each phrase, be sure to pause and feel how it "lands" for you; that is, rest in the result of cultivating each of these qualities as you say them:

  May I be filled with goodwill.

  Let me know well-being here and now.

  May I be able to connect to a sense of safety whenever I need it.

  Let me be guided by peace and ease.

  May I know true happiness all the days of my life.

- Now, take a deep breath and on the exhale just let yourself feel one or more of these qualities suffuse you, perhaps as a warmth, a wave, or any other sensation that flows through you. When you're ready, open your eyes if they've been closed.

- Using just one phrase or even just a key word per practice session can be a version of this practice.

Metta qualities are sometimes summarized simply as kindness. All the people I know who are kind have a gentleness to them. Thus, when we can connect to metta it softens us, first to our own suffering and then to that of others. It provides us with the gentleness that is so needed to be compassionate, to alleviate suffering with grace.

Metta "suffuses" not only more widely with the expansion from self to other, it also permeates. If we take on a consistent practice with metta (or any of the Brahma Viharas) for ourselves, it helps us change our thinking patterns by "reseeding" our field of awareness, as described in the Skillful Motivation chapter. This practice also doesn't have to be only when we're meditating. I encourage you to memorize metta and other Brahma Vihara phrases because they can be practiced in your daily life. For instance, when I'm waiting for the bus or other public transportation, instead of waiting impatiently, thinking "When is that bus coming?" I stop myself and, with mindful intention, redirect my thinking by saying the phrases. They can also be returned to in moments of stress or doubt as a way to recenter yourself in gentle self-kindness.

PRACTICE PAUSE

Off-the-Cushion Metta and Mala Practice

In Buddhism, a *mala* is a set of beads made to support recitation practice. Saying metta or other Brahma Viharas phrases is such a practice, as is reciting other mantras. Many people find that the physical action of using malas deepens their practice and aids concentration. Malas come in different sizes, but a very popular one is bracelet-size, so that it's easy to have with you.

When you're waiting for the bus, to cross a crosswalk, or perhaps before you check a digital device for messages, just pause, take a deep breath, and then say one or more of the phrases as you move the beads through your fingers. (Or try reaching for your mala beads to replace a habitual behavior like mindlessly checking your phone!)

- To practice, hold the beads in your hand draped around your four fingers so that one bead is between your thumb and the side of the index finger.

- Say a phrase, and as it ends, move one bead toward you.

- Repeat this with the same phrase or a series of memorized phrases, one bead at a time.

- As much as you can, let yourself feel the quality of the phrase as you're saying it. (Remember that if it's hard to "know" the quality in the moment, bringing your attention to a body location and allowing for any relaxation to happen there is a great way to embody that quality.)

- Do this for one full completion of the number of beads on your mala or until the wait, or lull in time you have, ends.

- You can use any beaded bracelet for this. "Official" Buddhist ones will often include one big bead so that your fingers "know" when you've completed a full round.

  As an impatient person, I have found this practice useful as a self-soothing tool. Additionally, after many years of doing it, I feel that the practice has lessened my impatience in general. Thus, these moments of "gardening" have indeed reconditioned the "seeds" of my field of awareness, allowing for kindness, well-being, safety, peace, ease, and happiness to grow and bloom.

  May it be the same for you.

Just like my sharing at the beginning of this section, metta and the other Brahma Viharas practices are aspirational practices and so opposite feelings or resistance to one or more of the qualities in the phrases can come up. Practicing them is like tenderizing our hearts. The four Brahma Viharas are like visitors knocking at our hearts' door, waiting to be let in: first into the foyer, then farther and farther into our house until they become good friends, ready to offer an arm or shoulder to lean on whenever you need support.

And like any tenderizing process, these practices take time to absorb. Oppression is pervasive and enduring. It can grind and fragment us. To protect ourselves from its forces, many of us become defensive, hardening against the pain, hurt, and harm of oppressions such as racism. As BIPOCs, to be able to have moments in which we can let down our guard and be able to express the fullness of our humanity is important. We can let ourselves reconnect to our own gentle nature.

S Is for Significant

Significant speech is communication that takes into account what is important for everyone in a conversation and is in service of connection. In the memory at the beginning of this chapter, the Abbot responded in a way that was significant for him, but it wasn't significant for me. I brought up what was significant for me, but he did not acknowledge it at all. A culture of domination such as white supremacy culture centers white people's points of view as what is important and valid. White privilege carries with it the sense that white people's points of view trump other races' points of view, and thus they feel entitled to decide or designate value to what topic carries more significance than another.

In the situation with the Abbot, I don't think that he didn't hear what I said, he simply deemed it as insignificant. He deemed what he wanted to talk about as more important than what I was sharing with him. As he was in the position of power—being the Abbot, male and white—he acted on the privileges he felt he was entitled to in those social locations of dominance.

I am aware that for many white-identified folks, especially born before the U.S. civil rights era or in less diverse areas, they were taught that to talk about race is to be racist, and so when it comes up, they ignore it. Perhaps that was what was going on for the Abbot. However, this only brings to the forefront the issue that more convert Buddhist settings need to better train teachers on antiracism and support and promote more teachers and leaders of color. As I write this book, if you take a look at the upper echelon of prominent convert centers and other institutions that teach and disseminate Buddhism in North America, they are still predominantly run by white people.

A crucial part of antiracism and anti-oppression work is to open up our sense of what is significant and valued. Our practice needs to actively and persistently emphasize becoming more aware of what is significant, especially in areas where we have been conditioned by white supremacy culture to ignore, deny, or minimize race and racism. For those in dominant positions, deep listening is a practice of not reacting from or centering one's point of view first and foremost. We can practice from a place of understanding that each of us inhabits our social location in the various systems of oppression and the resulting power differential each interaction carries.

○ ○ ○ ○

Depending on who is in the room and contexts such as gender, race, age, ability, sexual orientation, immigration status, neurodiversity, and so on, a person's location of privilege can shift and change. For instance, according to the Matrix of Domination, in the system of gender, as a woman, I am in the oppressed position. As an able-bodied person, I'm in a privileged location in the system of ableism.

We cannot ignore nor deny our locations since we live in these systems of oppression. We can want them to end. We can work for them to end. But right now they have not ended, and so our practice is to acknowledge that they are still continuing.

Our practice is actually to inhabit our social location with integrity, knowing both when it's useful to inhabit a particular location and when we need to be flexible and let go of imputed roles of a particular location. Suffering happens when we are insistent that others inhabit a location that we think they should inhabit or when we force ourselves to inhabit a location. Before coming out, I forced myself to be a certain way. Going on dates with men that I had no interest in was one such example.

In the system of white supremacy, whiteness or white culture is centered. I need to recenter as an Asian American, as a Vietnamese American. In the system of homophobia and heterosexism, we need to recenter what it means to love someone of a gender that's nonconforming, or recenter openness to gender diversity. We want to create a field in which other perspectives (especially nondominant ones) are also significant, are also given access, and are seen, heard, and valued. Skillful Speech, as the first of the Compassionate Conduct grouping of the Engaged Eightfold Path, offers us the tools to do so, recentering or shifting our communications to being based in qualities that support connection and context through the practices of TUGS: truthful, uplifting, gentle, and significant.

PART III

REALIZING THE WHOLENESS OF THE WORLD

8

SKILLFUL ENACTMENT
Wholeness with the
Interbeing Contract

I'M AT THE CHECK-OUT counter at my local general merchandise store. I'm with a new girlfriend, Tammy,* who is white. We have been dating for just about two weeks. This is our first shopping trip together to buy something for my apartment, where we plan to hole up for an intimate weekend.

We get to the counter, and, floating on cloud nine, barely pay any attention to the high beeps of our items getting scanned. The clerk bags the items, waiting for the total to come up on the screen.

"$19.37, please," the clerk relays.

I hand her my credit card and she runs it through the machine. She then tears the receipt off, places it on top of the credit card and gives it back to Tammy, saying, "Thank you," as she turns to the next customer.

Tammy takes the receipt and credit card and turns to walk away. I am still standing at the counter, trying to decide what to do. Then, noticing that Tammy has left, I follow her.

---

* To protect privacy, the name has been changed. "Tam" does mean "heart" in Vietnamese and is gender neutral.

Meeting up with Tammy, I am silent, my chest heavy and throat constricted before forcefully asking, "Didn't you see that?"

She looks baffled and answers, "What?"

I stalk away, fuming to myself.

○ ○ ○ ○

The second factor of the Compassionate Connection grouping of the Eightfold Path is classically called Skillful Action and is about practicing the Five
Precepts. In the Engaged version I'm reframing it as Skillful Enactment
because I want to emphasize *the commitment to apply* the Five Precepts in
our everyday life and antiracist work.

In Western convert settings, meditation is seen as the main aspect
of Buddhist practice. However, in most of the Buddhist world, which is
predominantly made up of Asian-heritage practitioners, it actually begins
and is grounded in the precepts. The precepts can be seen as essential
core values, and when you have studied and are living in accordance with
your values, then your heart and your mind are naturally more peaceful
and at ease before you go to do the mental training of meditative practices.

In different Buddhist sects, there are variations on the number or com-
binations of precepts. Additionally, often there is a differentiation between
the numbers and kinds for lay people versus monastics, even between the
monks and the nuns. However, the five of not killing, not stealing, not
misusing sexuality, not lying, and not intoxicating are agreed upon by all
the sects of Buddhism and practiced by everyone. I would even posit that
many other cultures besides Buddhist have some parameters around these
five because these are areas that carry the greatest potential to bring dis-
harmony or harm when we're not careful with them and we don't live in
awareness of their impact.

THE FIVE INTERBEING CONTRACTS

For our purposes, I'm calling the Five Precepts the Five Interbeing Contracts, as ways to honor each other and as an expression of our wholeness
in connections. Interbeing is not just between humans but with all beings,

including the Earth. In Zen we even practice relating to objects. For instance, we practice holding objects with two hands. This is not just to be hoity toity, though sometimes it may look like that; in general, the aim of the practice is to learn to be mindful and careful with objects as a way to then bring it into our interactions with all phenomena. Often our interactions with certain objects in a temple or practice setting carries meaning. For instance, when a priest offers incense, it is said that the smoke is carrying a wish or message to other realms, such as to the Buddha or ancestors. At their base, forms or ritualized parameters are set up as practices to support the awareness of how we are always in interaction with life.

Many of us Asian-heritage folks who were raised in Buddhist settings have been exposed to these precepts implicitly if not explicitly. Since Buddhism began almost 2,600 years ago, it often incorporates elements of Daoism, animism, and other cultural-based spirituality of whatever cultures it has traveled through. For many Asian-heritage people, and certainly for Asian immigrants like me, Buddhism was part of our everyday life. I remember a Vietnamese mentor of mine telling me about how, when she was a child back in Vietnam and spending time with her grandmother, she went to swat at a mosquito. Her grandmother said to her, "Remember, you're not separate from it." This was a teaching on not killing, to honor the interconnectedness of life.

In our working image of the Net of Indra, you could say that these Interbeing Contracts are commitments between the jewels to know that we are all dedicated to doing our part to uphold and maintain how the net supports us all. Because they are so fundamental, when one of these Interbeing Contracts is broken or damaged, the impact sends a strong reverberation throughout the strands, at times to the point of damaging the jewels. I can see this analogy applying to how incidents of racism fragment and damage the jewels. When one of the basic precepts is broken, I often feel shaken and discombobulated. Therefore, understanding and practicing in accordance with these five precepts is to live a life of wholeness.

As we study and practice with these precepts, we gain confidence that we *have the agency* to act from wholeness for ourselves as well as supporting others to connect to their own agency for wholeness. To do so is to foster and enact connections instead of egocentric individualism. Oppressive systems such as white supremacy culture disrupt these fundamental Interbeing Contracts. As a way to heal and restore from oppressive forces, we have to bring attention and commitment to how we're going to respond to their impacts on us. We have to make sure we don't respond in similarly harmful ways.

CAUSE AND EFFECT IN THE FOUR NOBLE TRUTHS

A way to support us to know we have agency to respond in nonharming ways is to view the Four Noble Truths as two pairs of effect (or result) and cause:

THE FOUR NOBLE TRUTHS	CORRESPONDING PRACTICE INSTRUCTIONS
Effect: Dukkha (harm and harming) exists (First Noble Truth)	to be **Investigated**
Cause: There is a cause or origins to dukkha (Second Noble Truth)	to be **Abandoned**
Effect: Cessation or alleviation of dukkha (Third Noble Truth)	to be **Realized**
Cause: The Eightfold Path leads to dukkha's cessation (Fourth Noble Truth)	to be **Developed**

For instance, imagine there has been a racial incident. This is the effect, experienced as the impact of harm or harming by racialization or racism. To know fully how this effect came into being, we investigate to understand the causes and conditions for how harm and harming came into being. By doing so, we understand its consequences, and so, ideally and with practice, it's easier to abandon harmful causes and conditions.

PRACTICE PAUSE

Investigating Effect and Cause

Let's apply this to the incident above at the store:

Effect of harm: The clerk handing the credit card receipt back to my girlfriend, Tammy, instead of me, even though it's my credit card.

Cause of harm: White supremacy culture's racist invisibilization of Asian Americans.

Effect to end harm: Cessation of the invisibilization of Asian Americans.

Cause to end harm: While not initially skillfully done in the above incident, drawing attention to the invisibilization is a way to hopefully bring a different cause to similar events in the future; that is, for my girlfriend to not unconsciously collude in perpetuating invisibilization of me. (As we'll see below, practicing Skillful Enactment intentionally can provide more skillful responses between me and my girlfriend.)

If you would like to try this out for yourself, apply these to an event in your life. Again, self-regulate by choosing a mild event and perhaps not even race-based if this is your first time with this exercise.

In practicing with this effect-and-cause framing, the important thing is to see that, when the result is harm and harming, **it came about because of an effect or result of something** *that came before.* This is crucial because it can give us hope for change. To me, using the framework above so clearly lays out the possibility of choice, of self-agency. Just like in my example, even if I'm clear about the causes of harm, when I went through the second pair of effect and cause, it helped me to see how my response to the incident, while addressing the harmful effects of white supremacy culture's invisibilizing of Asian Americans, was not in alignment with my own intentions to communicate or act from connection and wholeness. Thus, this framework can also provide us with a tool for evaluating if we have skillfully enacted our nonharming values.

Thus, if we want racial equality (a positive or skillful result), the second set shows us the possibility of strengthening individual and collective agency for ending harm and harming. Now we can see that by practicing the Engaged Eightfold Path, we can create the causes or conditions to enact this possibility.

Laid out in this way, we can see how critical the practice instructions are for each Noble Truth. When there's harm and harming, the practice instruction is to investigate. Part of investigating is to acknowledge, or clearly discern and agree on what the issue is. In fact, before we can even address an issue, we have to acknowledge and mutually agree that a certain effect has happened. When all parties can agree to a clear sense or definition of a problem, then the investigation's purpose becomes more directed and focused. Otherwise, the investigation can be full of misguided energy and effort, resulting in further misdirection or confusion. We investigate to know the causes and conditions that have brought about an issue or problem. Once we know them, we need to abandon them. That's the practice instruction of the Second Noble Truth.

In reconciliation or restoration, when there has been hurt or harm done, it isn't enough to just say, "Sorry." For any meaningful healing and restoration to happen, there also has to be a commitment and a plan of actions to not repeat the same harm and causes of harm again. With this formatting of the Engaged Four Noble Truths, we can see the Third and Fourth Noble Truths as the *positive* form of effect and cause: if we want nonharming to be the effect, then developing the Eightfold Path is the cause, or means, to do so. The Third Noble Truth practice instruction is "to be realized."

In Buddhism, "realizing" does involve taking in information and acquiring knowledge, but it also is about how you put it into action. When we understand what can be nonharming, we also have to enact it by practicing the Engaged Eightfold Path. As we practice the eight factors and see the results of less and less harm to ourselves and others, then it strengthens our trust, faith, and confidence in the Third Noble Truth. I know I feel most defeated and disempowered when I don't have a sense of a lessening or ending of dukkha, of harm and harming.

Luckily for us, as we've been learning with our studies in this book, the Eightfold Path lays out for us what is nonharming *and* gives us skillful means to do so. In many ways, our practice is to strengthen the second pairing of effect and cause. I practice to know that it's possible for me to have confidence that I can alleviate or end harm through my practice of the Eightfold Path.

○ ○ ○ ○

To me, the word *enactment* also encompasses having my practice be so integrated that I'm committed to *acting* from knowing that it's possible to realize nonharming. In Mahayana Buddhist philosophy, of which Zen is a part, you could say that we begin with the Third Noble Truth. We start with the belief that each of us is born endowed with Buddha nature, the capacity all beings have to be Buddhas, to know and live as fully awake in the wholeness of life. It is said that Dogen, the Japanese founder of Soto Zen, hearing this, then wondered, "If that's true, then why should I practice?" After many years of practice with this question as his koan, he realized that enlightenment and practice are not two separate things. He came up with the term "practice-realization." As we practice, we realize that enlightenment, or awakening, to our interconnectedness with life is right here. In practicing we're simultaneously enacting awakening to wholeness. Knowing this intellectually is fine, but it's hard to continuously act from this in a sustained way; thus we have to keep on practicing.

I also like the word *enactment* because it reflects that I'm putting into action a purpose I have. It highlights that the action I'm going to take is based on a motivation that is choiceful and not reactive. Additionally, when activated, policies and laws are "enacted," so this word also brings with it the framing of a systemic act of restoration or upholding of a set of values we have with each other.

The Five Precepts offer us guidance to practice and a means to build confidence that we are enacting our values to make and sustain connections toward the cause of nonharming and wholeness. In fact, I think they give us a way to know we can be aware and act with agency and that there's always a choice on how to respond from our awakened, whole, complete Buddha nature.

LIVING THE FIVE PRECEPTS
(AKA INTERBEING CONTRACTS)

Before we go through each of the precepts individually, I want to share why they are classically framed in the negative. By putting the precepts in a "not" format, it gives a very clear container for appropriate behavior. "Not killing" provides a container to ask yourself, "If or when I do this, am I killing or not killing?" But of course life, especially lay life, is complex, because we interact with all kinds of people in all kinds of contexts in which there is often not just one clear set of mutually agreed-on values or how to be accountable to them.

Even among different Buddhist communities, how strict the precepts are adhered to depends on lineages' norms and cultural contexts. For instance, I know from practicing in several monasteries of the Thai Forest Tradition that, while monastics cannot directly kill or praise killing, since they are mendicants and going on alms rounds is their only means of obtaining food, they must receive what is given. Additionally, for many Thais, meat is considered a luxury. As a result, believing that giving the best of what you have to a monastic brings the greatest merit, even the poorest people will strive to offer meat as a way of practicing dedicated generosity.

As the "not" version can bring with it a too-rigid sense of morality, framing the precepts in a positive way can offer us inspiration. Sometimes when we know we have not acted well and get stuck in beating ourselves up with remorse, it's useful to remember the aspirational intentions of the precepts as a way to inspire us to rededicate ourselves to them in a fresh way.

Therefore, I'll frame the precepts in both negative and positive frames as we briefly go through them.

Not Killing/Honoring Life

It is said in Buddhism that if all the precepts collapse down into one, it would be the precept of not killing. If I had to say what Buddhism is in one word, it would be "nonharming." Besides the understanding of this as strictly not killing, it is useful to see this precept as about what kind of energy we want to promote with our actions: enlivening or deadening? This is how the positive framing of the precepts really supports our studies of antiracism. We honor life when we bring awareness to where we've been taught, explicitly or implicitly, to not pay attention or notice when harm has occurred. This also directs us toward how our unconsciousness can be a form of harming.

When we make assumptions about others, the result is often harmful, although unconsciously. This is why mindfulness of thinking can be framed as the practice of becoming more aware of our implicit bias. For Asian Americans, one area of implicit bias that is present in many of our communities is anti-Blackness. When we acknowledge that anti-Blackness exists, then we can move to action to address this harm and work at coalition building between our communities.

Not Stealing or Noncovetousness/ Sharing or Contentment

Not stealing is often also framed as "not taking what is not freely given," or not taking something unless it's freely offered. This is a useful framing for working with identifying privilege and entitlement. Entitlement is believing that I have a right to something whether it was given to me or not.

For instance, I became a vegan as a way to practice the Buddhist precept of not-killing. My girlfriend, as an animal rights person, helped me to see how it's also a practice of not taking what is not given. From her, I was able to see that being vegan is not just about not eating animals. Wool and honey are parts of the animal that they have not freely given to us. Sheep are bred to produce fur that's beyond what's natural for them. These animals suffer from being bred to grow excessive hair to the point in which it's so heavy that they can't support themselves. At times they are unable to move and are left to wallow in their own waste, causing sores and more unnecessary pain and illnesses. When honey is taken from beehives, they are given sugar water instead. Honey is their natural nutrient-rich food, so replacing it with sugar water has been proven to bring disease to the hives to the point of killing them all.[1] Additionally, this is robbing them of the product of their labor.

On the human scale, we know that many Indigenous cultures have a basis of generosity and sharing, and so the sense of property and ownership is open and inclusive. Of course, the most obvious example of how this was taken advantage of is when Europeans first came to the continent of what we now call North America and assumed ownership of this land by framing it as "discovery of the New World." Imperial and colonial mindsets are based on imputing inferiority onto individuals, peoples, or cultures they want to seize. Thus dogmas such as Manifest Destiny, the "God-given" right to expand across the continent, was used by the U.S. government in the mid-1800s to justify the taking of Indigenous peoples' land, manipulating Indigenous peoples' cultural idea of sharing to the European colonial-based mind-set of ownership. The United States, by participating in Europeans' ideology of North American frontiers as being territory to be "owned" by the countries of Europe, colluded with and then took on this mind-set. This led then to the justification of wars and "relocating" of Indigenous people such as the Comanche people from large areas of the West to reservations in Oklahoma.[2]

Buddhism also begins with generosity as its basis. *Dana,* the Pali word for "generosity" or "freely given," shows up as the beginning of many of the Buddha's lists of core practices. For the laity, the list of practices includes dana (generosity), *shila* (ethical conduct, or compassionate conduct in the Engaged Four Noble Truths version), and *bhavana* (meditation).

At the nunnery where I practiced in Vietnam, nothing was owned by an individual. When I entered the nunnery as a guest monastic, I was given two sets of clothing. Each day, right after lunch, just before afternoon rest, I would wash one set and then hang it up to dry during nap time. It dried easily because it was made of thin cloth, and it was breezy in Da Lat, considered the "mountainous" area in central Vietnam and known for its temperate climate. I was also given two bowls, a pair of chopsticks, and a spoon. I did have my name on them, but only so that I was responsible for washing them myself after every meal. When I left the nunnery, I returned them to be used by another nun after me. All food, hygiene products, and other belongings were provided. All donations, even when given on a one-to-one basis, were then given to the storage nun, and she redistributed them to everyone as needed.

In this Vietnamese tradition, they are essentially vegan. They do not buy eggs, butter, or cheese, but if it is given, as a form of alms-receiving, they will accept it and eat it. In Vietnam, Laughing Cow cheese is very popular. It is a round box of pasteurized soft white cheese with six sections individually wrapped inside. It came with the French when they colonized Vietnam. Now, it is part of Vietnamese culture and foods, eaten as a popular snack with bananas or as a quick to-go breakfast sandwich: a few wedges stuffed into a small baguette (another remnant of French colonization).

While there, I heard a story about a nun whose family came to visit. Everyone knew no one was allowed to receive anything personal, but of course parents know what you like, so they gave her a box of Laughing Cow cheese. She kept it to herself but did give a wedge to one of her friends in her residence area.

At this nunnery, once a month on the full moon, they have a repentance meeting, where the nuns go and repent how they have broken the precepts that month. At that month's repentance meeting, this nun felt bad that she had kept the box of Laughing Cow cheese so she confessed her covetousness. At first, hearing the story, I thought it was a bit silly, taking this precept of noncovetousness too far. But with time, I recognized this was about to what degree we are willing to practice our values.

If we say that our practice is open generosity and have entered into an agreement to live sharing resources with all, then are we willing to really practice that continuously? That's the difficulty with practicing the precepts. In general, the more we practice with them, the more we see where and how we may not be acting in accordance with our values. How committed are you to the container of sharing? Each of us has to make these decisions for ourselves and in context.

The precepts offer us an opportunity to become aware to what degree we are willing to live a life that quiets our hearts and minds. That is the standard to which we evaluate our behavior.

When someone has taken the precepts, we often think of them as trustworthy, and it's more than just an intellectual knowing. For me, there's a felt sense of settledness and quiet in heart, mind, and body when we live more and more in accordance with our values. I think this is why monasteries and retreat centers are places that many animals are drawn to. There is a peacefulness and sense of acceptance that develops as we practice hour after hour, day after day, creating an energetic field of settledness because we are in alignment with the integrity of our values and our behavior.

Not Misusing Sexuality/Honoring Connection and Intimacy

Classically, this means celibacy for monastics because the acts of sex are considered very passion-making and can then propel us into actions that are rash or extreme. However, another way to frame sexual urges is that it is about connecting to our life force. When this is applied to our interactions with others, it can be about intimacy and connection. To practice with this precept is to ask ourselves: How are my sexual feelings and behavior in alignment with connection and intimacy? Are my behaviors agreed upon by all involved? Are we fostering more intimacy and connection, or disrupting or violating connection and intimacy?

To what level do you take this to? Blanche, my teacher, loved to tell this story about a Benedictine monk who came to practice with Suzuki Roshi. In his Christian tradition, he had taken a vow of celibacy and when asked about it he replied, "But if I want to love everyone the same, I have to be either celibate or very promiscuous!" Blanche then said, "I love that image of loving everyone the same. That's something I've taken on myself, to love everyone the same, to love everyone completely."[3]

Of course, this is a story about the aspiration of open, freely given love and intimacy. Just like with the precept around killing, sexual intimacy is an area in which much harm can be caused if we don't act from connection and wholeness. In our daily life, it's important to remember that to not misuse sexuality includes practicing engaging in open and clear communications to honor and negotiate consensual boundaries for everyone involved in any relationship.

Not Lying or No False Speech/Promoting Truth

By framing this precept in the positive as promoting truth, it takes into account making access for truth-telling from many perspectives. I talked about this with Skillful Speech before as shifting or recentering speech to include more voices and points of view of oppressed groups, and therefore, increasing our understanding of the many truths in any situation. While I don't claim to speak for all Asians practicing, writing this book became a promotion of truth. The invisibilization of Asian Americans in general, and in North American convert Buddhism in particular, is so pervasive that the more I researched when formulating this book, the more I saw how few books there are on these topics from an Asian American perspective. I became more convinced that a book such as this needed to be written. As a generally introverted person, putting myself forward for causes has been a means for learning to engage my agency to speak up.

A school system's willingness to have a broader, inclusive history curriculum is a structural example of how we can be willing to promote more truths. Similarly, when white-centered practice places plaster their websites with photos of people of color while actually having few BIPOCs in their practice community or as teachers and staff, this is not truthful.

Not Intoxicating/Maintaining Clear Heart and Mind

Traditionally this precept is written as "not intoxicating with substances" and was specifically directed at alcohol and drugs. The main reason for this is that these substances alter our mental and emotional state and prevent us from seeing clearly. Using them, especially excessively, tends to increase our chances of making poor choices, especially in our behavior with others. It often increases saying or doing things we'll regret later or that can cause great harm.

When framed as "maintaining clear heart and mind," this precept asks us to observe what we're doing that takes us away from being fully present, especially with emotional difficulties within ourselves or in conflicts with others. Thus, any habitual way of diverting our attention in a compulsive way is considered a form of intoxication. Working to the point of disrupting relationships or life balance could be a form of intoxication. Checking your email or social media all the time could be considered intoxicating, or binge-watching a streaming series to the point that it negatively impacts your life. Even using meditation and other Buddhist practices as a means to turn away from or deny internal or external difficulties can be a form of intoxication.

PRACTICING WITH THE
FIVE PRECEPTS AND RACIAL INCIDENTS

Here are two examples of racist incidents I've experienced and how the five precepts can be applied to them. The five precepts may be in a different order than typically written to show the progression of thinking or actions in a more organic way. This is by no means an exhaustive list, nor should it be seen as the one and only "correct" way to apply how the precepts can be used as a guide to understanding racial dynamics, antiracist actions, or racial healing or restoration. However, specificity in real-life experiences and real-life responses can be useful as a way to show subtleties and nuances. These are offered as such.

Theme: Invisibility

Asian Americans are often the invisible minority in the United States. We are not included in many research projects or lists of statistics about race issues and race equity. This also plays out on a personal level. The first example relates to the memory of going to the store with my girlfriend that began this chapter. Refer to it as I apply the five precepts as a guide toward wholeness and connection.

- **I am killing/breaking connection** when I get mad at my partner for taking the credit card receipt instead of interrupting the invisibilization that's happening at the moment. Also, I saw how my reaction was killing self-connection (to the impact on me of being the target of racism; more on this below) and a deeper connection to my partner.

- **Not intoxicating.** I realized the anger at my girlfriend was an intoxication of anger, expressed as misplaced self-righteousness maxims: "She 'should' know better! She should have noticed! White people just don't understand! They're clueless!" I can intoxicate myself with my anger about what my girlfriend "should know," *or* I can attend to my hurt and sadness at not being seen. This leads to the next precept.

- **Not stealing/honoring sharing.** In not honoring my own experience as significant enough to share (especially the vulnerability of being the target of racism), I "stole" an opportunity for us to develop further intimacy. I did not want to show my pain of not being seen. I also did not share my experience of pain because I was afraid of losing the bond we were developing. As we were just starting to get to know each other, I was afraid it might cause tension and I would lose the intimacy we were developing. Yet in finally talking about it and being able to practice with it several more times, we actually built a deeper intimacy around this issue. When I went straight to anger, I also stole an opportunity to be with and attend to my own hurt and sadness.

- **Not misusing sexuality/Honoring connection and intimacy.** Sharing how painful such incidents of invisibilization are to me can build intimacy and trust, especially when I include my girlfriend on how we could mitigate similar incidents in the future. For example, she could not take the change or credit card when it's offered to her. She could point out the mistake to the employee.

Being able to share my full experience around this (and many other similar instances) with my girlfriend, I'm also allowing her to express her love and compassion so that the trust and intimacy we build is cocreated.

- **Promoting truth.** When I'm able to share the fullness of my experience—the frustrated anger that this is a repeated event I face often *and* the sadness that comes with being personally not seen—then I'm both giving voice to and honoring my truth. In sharing my experience with my girlfriend, I'm also opening the field for us both to feel brave and safe to share our truths with each other.

Theme: Target of Active Racism

Once, I rented a small apartment at the back of a house in a midsize West Coast college town. After having been there for a week I received a note tucked into the door jamb which read: "People like you should not live in this neighborhood." It was not signed. Fear and alarm came first, then anger at being watched and threatened.

- The note *killed* **a sense of safety.** It activated a sense of not being safe and I slept with a knife under my pillow for many months.

- But I did not let the note *steal* **my contentment.** I worked to not be overcome or ruled by the threat of its message by . . .

- **Honoring Connection to myself:** I stayed connected to myself by honoring my feelings and being with the fear brought up by the note.

- **Not Lying/Honoring Truth:** Showing the note to friends, I did not diminish the alarming nature of the note. Two close friends stayed the night with me. For a while they would walk me home to make sure I got in safely. I also was very much part of the college's student unions and got support there. Perhaps, the only "unskill-fulness" was that I never reported it to the police. I think it was because I had enough mirroring and people who understood my experience. By reaching out for help, I also **honored my connection** to others.

- **Nonintoxication/Clear Heart-Mind.** By taking the actions above, I was able to reestablish clarity of emotions and equanimity instead of letting fear and anger be the ruling emotions behind how I responded to the threat.

How can we live a life not overwhelmed by hate, greed, and delusion that is directed at us, our communities, and the planet? Bringing awareness and enactment of our individual and collective values reminds us of our interconnectedness. Taking the precepts is available to everyone. In fact, in Buddhism, you become a Buddhist when you take the precepts publicly in a ceremony. In many convert Buddhist centers, there isn't much emphasis on taking the precepts as a practice in and of itself, but its essence is there when the precepts are recited at the formal beginning of a retreat.

To practice the precepts is a deep and enduring commitment. In my tradition of Soto Zen, when a practitioner is ready to take the precepts publicly with a teacher, they have to formally ask three times. Then, there is a study period with that teacher. I offer precepts studies to my students once a year, for eight months. A part of that practice or study is to see the complexity of the precepts, and over this length of time, see how they apply in one's life.

When a person has taken the precepts, you know that they're committed to not killing, not stealing, not misusing sexuality, not lying, and not intoxicating as ways to protect themselves from doing harm when careless in these five areas. They become safer for you also. This is why communities who have taken the precepts are committing their whole lives to living by the precepts. As the precepts are available for everyone, practicing Skillful Enactment is a way of asking yourself, How much will I let the five Interbeing Contracts guide my life? In practicing them, how can I gain confidence that I have the agency to promote and act in nonharming ways?

SKILLFUL LIVING
A Life of Integrated Wholeness

IN THE 1990s, in my mid-twenties, I worked at a confidential domestic violence shelter, a house in an undisclosed location that accommodated up to seventeen women and their children. It was a white feminist organization trying to become multicultural. When I came onto the staff, they achieved their 50-50 goal of three white women and three people of color, with two Black women and me as their first and only Asian American.

About three months into my tenure, I was in the weekly staff meeting. The graveyard staff person, just getting off her shift, told us about a conflict that had happened earlier that morning. A Vietnamese woman with two kids had fried a pack of bacon for breakfast. As was common practice in the house, she shared it with anyone who wanted it, in this case, with a Black woman and her three children. The two women had become friends during their stay at the shelter and they all enjoyed the food together. That is, until there were just a few pieces left and they realized that this was the last of the bacon with no more packs to cook.

The Black woman said that the remaining bacon should go to her family because it was "Black people food." The Vietnamese woman wanted to continue to share it, but the Black woman took it all for her family and now the two women were mad at each other.

After relaying the events, the staff person said that as a Black person, she agreed with the Black client so she thought we needed to tell people that Black women should get the last pack of bacon if the issue came up again.

I voiced my disagreement, saying that pork was the most widely used meat in Vietnam. I also brought up a rule that is considered one of the "golden rules" specific to domestic violence shelters: no parameters around what, when, how much, or the timeframe when women eat or feed their children. This is because a common control tactic used by perpetrators in domestic violent relationships is to regulate food: cooking it in the "wrong way" or at the "wrong time" could be used as rationalization for beatings; denial of food or forced eating of rotten or nonhuman foods are also common.

The three white staff members, who had stayed frozen and silent all this time, joined in the discussion at this point and it was voted that we could not regulate who "owns" which foods.

As I was the day person who came on after this graveyard staff person, we would often talk with each other about many issues during our shift transition debriefings. She was an older woman, had worked at the shelter longer than me, and was the staff person I had the most one-on-one contact with. I had looked up to her as a mentor and friend. At our next meeting a few days later, after we had talked about shift transition issues, she said she wanted to talk about the bacon issue with me. I agreed, thinking it would be another bonding moment.

She started by asking me, "Why do you act like a white girl?" I was completely taken aback and stunned at such a racially insensitive statement by a coworker of color. With my heart racing and trying to be open to such an accusatory statement, I asked what she meant by it. She replied that I should have backed her up in the staff meeting since we're both people of color. She then said that I must have acted the way I did because I was adopted by white people and, therefore, could "act white."

Flabbergasted and hurt, I disagreed with her reasoning. As I began to bring up the reasons for the points of view I shared at yesterday's meeting, she then stated that Black people were more oppressed than Asians so, as Asians, we should always concede to Black people. Completely dismayed, I disagreed with her and shared that for me, racism impacts each group in different ways.

Neither of us shifted our points of view, and the encounter ended. After this, my relationship with the graveyard staff person never regained the intimacy of connection it had before.

○ ○ ○ ○

Skillful Living is classically called Skillful Livelihood. And while many of us spend a large amount of our time in work, it's not just about what kinds of employment are skillful or not. By using "Skillful Living," my aim is to focus more on the quality of how we are living our lives. This factor of the Eightfold Path can be about how we integrate all we've learned on the Path to keep living in wholeness and connection.

For instance, I hadn't thought about that staff meeting until the writing of this book. This surprised me because I thought it was settled. But when we've been in a difficult racial interaction, it often sticks with us. We can have tension in our body from various layers of reactions. Anxiety can make our stomach churn. We can have heartache from confusion for how a connection didn't happen or was lost. Often, we turn the interaction over and over again in our minds in an endless loop. Rethinking what we said or didn't say can bring judgment and shameful feelings for how we "should have" expressed ourselves in the situation.

The staff meeting at the shelter was an example of the complexity of race interactions in the United States. For many of us, racial interactions are difficult, painful, often harmful, and can leave us feeling unsettled and unresolved. However, we are rarely shown how to hold the complexity of body, heart, and mind after complicated racial interactions. We are not often given tools for how to *be with* the aftermath of such interactions. We're not often trained to process them in ways that provide enough relief to let it rest so that it doesn't overly determine future interactions.

This is the truth for many of us living in the system of white supremacy culture in North America. It feels charged. It feels complicated. It feels too scary. It brings isolation and distance when, in fact, connection is what we're after. This was certainly how I felt about my experience at that staff meeting and the resulting interaction after.

It has taken me almost thirty years to have a more complete sense of how to hold that experience in a way that wasn't mostly just confusion and hurt. As indicated earlier, the years of activism and professional work as a social worker certainly provided critical race theory learning and application within a social justice framework. Therapy and years of Buddhist practices provided broad stability and wisdom on the nature of suffering, distress, dis-ease, and challenge. But it was only through the schematics of the Engaged Four Noble Truths in the realm of antiracism as a response to these recent years of national and world crises, that the events of that staff meeting now make more sense to me in ways that can bring closure. With the Engaged perspective, I can see how all of us at that staff meeting acted from our various social locations within the system of white supremacy culture, driven by unexamined beliefs, scripted by conditioned reactive habits of communication and behavior.

I wonder, if I had been grounded in these Engaged Truths' framing and their practices then, would I have been able to find ways to stay intimate with that graveyard staff person? If the white staff members had also practiced with these Truths, would they have been more participatory right away, so that the staff meeting would have been more of a fully engaged discussion and less of the POC-on-POC dialogue? Of course, we all have our own ways of making sense of ourselves and our relationships to each other and the world. I hope every staff member at the shelter has not "carried" this staff meeting with them for as long as I have! And if they have, may they have found their own resolution to it.

For me, having these Truths has supported me to connect to and use qualities of mindful attention and compassionate responses to my own hurt and pain in ways that supported healing and restoration for myself, and with it, wholeness-centered engagement in all facets of my life.

TENDING TO THE NET

At this point in the book, I hope you, too, have been able to use the wisdom and the tools from the Engaged Four Noble Truths and Engaged Eightfold Path.

While individual healing is important and a necessary step, given how it's emphasized in North American–dominant culture generally, and within white-dominant convert Buddhist practices in particular, this book has emphasized the structural and systemic conditions of white supremacy culture and its effects on practitioners of Asian heritage in particular, and on all practitioners interested in incorporating antiracist and social justice into their practice. In this book, we have focused on the Net of Indra—the whole net, not just the jewels—as a way to see the strands as the systems and structures that *can* provide a sense of the wholeness of the net as strong, solid, mutual connections between and among jewels. We have also seen how, when the strands are not attended to, consciously by systems of oppression such as racism or unconsciously by individuals and communities conditioned by those systems, not only is the net not healthy but the jewels are also harmed.

At this time, we want to consider ways we can think of the net as complete. While we have concentrated on the strands due to individual-focused conditioning, we also want to remember that the jewels are part of the net. Net and jewels are together; they are not mutually exclusive.

Liberation is to wake up to how we've been unconscious. This begins with fully acknowledging where there are breaks in the system or within ourselves. The Engaged Four Noble Truths support us to see how wholeness may not have been known because we haven't opened ourselves up to seeing it. We can have a larger view by examining how we were conditioned by our family, cultures, systems, and national and world history.

There's a saying in Zen that delusion and enlightenment are intertwined; they are not separate. Recently, I had an experience that exemplified this for me very clearly. I was at the Russian River, where there's a lot of nature, including many spiderwebs on the railing of the back porch of the house where I was staying. In the spring, there are also many dandelion puffs on the lawn. The puffiness of these heads is from the white fluffy tuft of hair on each dandelion seed, called a pappus. One day, as I looked out, there were so many of these pappi floating in the air that it looked like it was snowing! These pappi were getting caught in the webs on the back porch. Because of the thinness of the strands of a spiderweb, sometimes it can be hard to see the web itself unless you look at it from the right angle or the light is just right. However, because of this "snow," the webs on the back porch were easily visible. I didn't have to search for them. It was very obvious that they were there.

A spiderweb is often used as a representation of the Net of Indra. Dandelions are considered a "weed" and so are often thought of as bad or not wanted. We often are taught the same about dukkha, our pain and suffering: that they should not be, and therefore are to be gotten rid of when present. Many of us come to practice to get rid of pain and suffering as opposed to examining how we can investigate the possible messages they signal. And yet, when conditions are appropriate and we are able to see a weed, or dukkha, *in context,* there can be healing in that moment. If we only see dukkha, such as the hurt and harm of racism, as something to be gotten rid of, then we miss the opportunity to see how, when we can be with and investigate dukkha, it can be a means to healing and restoration. As stated before, how much a hurt is experienced as a harm is dependent on how the hurt was, or is, held and processed. Dukkha, then, when framed in contexts that include skillful means and appropriate support, such as is offered by the Engaged Four Noble Truths and its Eightfold Path factors, can be transformed into ways to let go or be released from the harm it has caused. This is a moment of healing and restoration. Such a moment is freedom from suffering and those old causes of suffering: the message offered to us by the Third Noble Truth. Hurt and harm, when viewed and practiced within contexts that are meaningful to us, can be the fodder for growth and transformation. Thus, what was "a weed," a hurt that was not attended to previously, when held in contexts that make sense to us now, can be the means that show us what was already here: the connections in life. The pappi, in the transformational newness of spring, helps us to see the net, or wholeness, easily.

Dogen wrote that those who think they're enlightened are deluded, and those who know they are deluded are enlightened.[1]

When we see our delusion, *that* is a moment of enlightenment. We are deluded if we think and act *not* with the wholeness of the net in mind. We are not isolated beings. We wake up to knowing that being supported and supporting are interconnected. Living centered by our values, such as the Interbeing Contract (Five Precepts), is a way we can know that we are being supported and, in practicing them, that we support others. When we don't live with a centering set of values, it can result in dysfunction. When the resulting degree of dysfunction comes to a critical mass, it can actually show us that wholeness is already possible right here and now *if* we're paying attention at such a moment. Additionally, if we're willing to work to rectify the dysfunctions, we can realize that as jewels, we're actually here being supported by—and are ourselves the stewards of—the net.

THE THREE LAYERS OF ABSORPTION

The Engaged Four Noble Truths and the Engaged Eightfold Path give us the framing and tools to be stewards of the net. The Noble Truths have three layers of absorption: understanding, practicing, and realizing. If you're surprised by this, don't worry; we've been doing them this whole time! Let's see how.

Understand

The first level of absorption is to understand the teachings of what suffering and harming are. This involves reading and studying sutras and their commentaries. We do need to have some intellectual knowledge about the framework for how to observe and investigate suffering. Memorizing and understanding lists and practice instructions, such as the components of the Engaged Four Noble Truths or the steps of PACE, are also examples of implementing this layer.

Another way to understand the Dharma is to read explanations on the teachings, especially ones that are applied to everyday life situations, such as books like this one. Listening to Dharma talks, taking classes or studying with a teacher, or having discussions on teaching points with other practitioners are other ways to understand the Dharma and its relevance to your life. In Soto Zen, we also emphasize regular meetings with a teacher as a way to keep clarifying your understanding.

Practice

Next comes putting the teachings into practice. We have been doing this by applying the Engaged Four Noble Truths' framing of harm and harming (First Engaged Noble Truth), the causes and conditions for their arising and continuation (Second Engaged Noble Truth), how agency and restoration is possible (Third Engaged Noble Truth), and then how that possibility can be achieved through skillfully practicing the Eightfold Path factors (Fourth Engaged Noble Truth). In particular, we focused the application of these teachings to how we are racialized and the impact of race oppression and white supremacy culture. When you practiced any of the meditative, reflective writing or mindfulness Practice Pauses offered in this book, you were engaging in this layer. Chanting, recitation (of metta phrases, for example), bowing, and offering incense or other forms in temples or in our homes are other ways of practicing to enact the teachings.

Realize

Hopefully, as you've been going through this book, you have also started to integrate the teachings and practices into your life. This is the realizing layer. "Realizing" doesn't necessarily mean exalted states. As you're practicing, you're integrating, and as you're integrating, you're realizing. Experiential knowledge is the highest form of knowing in Buddhism. When there is congruence between your understanding and practice of the teachings with how you think, feel, and behave, then you're realizing. When we integrate wholeness so that it becomes embodied and there's no separation, then we're realizing.

By going through the Eightfold Path steps in this book, you've been offered ways to know, understand, and practice the Engaged Four Noble Truths as teachings that both define *and* give guidance on how to live a life of nonharming. When jewel and net are not mutually exclusive, then you're realizing a life dedicated to wholeness.

bell hooks, in her essay "Contemplation and Transformation" from *Buddhist Women on the Edge,* says, "A culture of domination like ours says to people: There is nothing in you that is of value; everything of value is outside you and must be acquired. This is the message of devaluation."[2]

White supremacy culture's machination hurts and harms us individually and collectively through othering, bringing with it messages, interactions, policies, and laws that seek to fragment and even destroy us in body, heart, mind, and spirit. Thus, our work is also that of self-repair, self-restoration, and reclaiming a wholeness that is inherent in each of us.

At some point we have to be conscious to value ourselves and then find practices to support this. To me, healing from the hurt and harm of racism is what I call reclaiming, or returning, to wholeness—to a sense of completeness, to a sense of the fullness of life. In Mahayana Buddhism, we believe that all beings are born with inherent wholeness, which we call *buddha-dhatu,* or Buddha nature. Classically, Buddha nature is a being's capacity for awakening. The word *buddha* comes from the word *bodhi,* which means "to awaken." You already have the capacity to awaken as part of your being.

Buddha nature can also be seen as living in wholeness, living with a sense of completeness, not only in ourselves but also with life. It is about a unified sense of wholeness that is possible for you, me, and for all of us to know and connect to. To awaken to our Buddha nature is to awaken to a unified sense in each of us, between us, and with all that connects us. It is the whole net.

○ ○ ○ ○

My girlfriend does freelance documentary work and recently did a story about benitoite. Benitoite is the state gem of California. Specifically, it is found in San Benito County, so it was named after that place. Other places like Japan and Norway have some, but they're very small pieces. San Benito is the only place that is known to have substantial quantities and pure qualities of benitoite that are big enough to make jewels out of. A unique property of benitoite is that it has double refraction, which means that when light hits it, the rays break into two. Thus, benitoite sparkles even brighter than diamonds! The gem is made when the specific chemicals inherent to benitoite are present while two tectonic plates rub against each other.

Similarly, our practice is like where the two plates meet and friction happens. There's lots of rubbing. It is because of that friction that our beauty is revealed. By this, I don't mean that we must have friction or conflict for our beauty to become apparent, more that it does tend to take being able to be with dis-ease and discomfort on the journey toward such revelation. Perhaps as you have been reading this book, you have thought at some point, "This is way too hard. I did not sign up for this!" I have hope that even though it's been difficult, that it has really shown you that you are jewels *within* the net. Whatever fragmentation, chipping, or rubbing off has happened due to systems of oppression such as racism—it hasn't destroyed or broken you. In fact, it can be restorative to see that we have agency to define and heal ourselves.

As jewels, we need to awaken to knowing that we are not separate from the net; you are already an integral part of wholeness and completeness. In fully knowing this, we realize that we all are stewards of the net, living in peace and harmony with all beings. Skillful Living, then, is the commitment to bring all that we've discovered on the Path to enact wholeness from this day forth, in our lives and in antiracist work.

CONCLUSION

Wholeness Is Here, Home Is Here

MY HEARTBEAT POUNDED LOUDLY in my ears as I nervously waited to be interviewed to find out if I could join a nunnery in Da Lat, Vietnam, for five days of guest practice. I was back in Vietnam for the second time since leaving as a child in 1973. This was the third leg of my journey of overseas Buddhist practice that had begun in Japan and continued in Thailand before coming here. I had heard about this popular Vietnamese Zen tradition called Truc Lam, or Bamboo Forest, from a Vietnamese American friend in the United States. I was eager to try this practice as an expansion of my Buddhist practice.

It was barely sunrise as I stood waiting inside the main room of the guest house. I was especially nervous because my Vietnamese is very poor. In the thirty-two years since I had left as an adoptee at the age of eight, I had tried to relearn Vietnamese numerous times, listening to language tapes, taking various kinds of classes, and working one-on-one with tutors. And still, I could barely speak it, not even the child Vietnamese many of my friends in the United States spoke. While it was true that this second time back to Vietnam was not as emotionally loaded as the first time four years before, my nervousness at having to speak Vietnamese only increased with the prospect of having to interview to be accepted. Last time, in 2002, I had come "to move back home," having felt I was "taken" from my home country since I didn't have a choice as a child. But, after five months of immersion, I had left feeling very much "a foreigner," as I never felt like I fit in. Ironically, it is only in Vietnam that I am thought of as "too American," or not Vietnamese enough.

Finally, a senior teacher came to interview me. Luckily, her English was much better than my Vietnamese, and she had a kind gentle manner. After asking a series of questions about when I was ordained and about my monastic experiences, she informed me I would be taken to meet the Abbess and the Vice Abbess for the final approval.

With sweat dripping down my back that was not all about the heat of the day increasing with the rising of the sun, I followed her out the door of the guest house. My mind kept looping over and over the general Vietnamese greeting of *"Chao Co,"* or "Greetings, (Miss) Nun," trying to get the proper tonal qualities that made Vietnamese especially hard for me. We passed nuns busily sweeping and attending to the lush potted plants, some staring openly at us, others sneaking surreptitious glances.

We arrived at the Abbess's quarters, and I was introduced by the teacher who had interviewed me. I bowed deeply but kept silent as they continued talking. Then the interviewing nun said, "The Abbess is asking, 'Do you know you have Buddha nature?'" I was floored. I had expected a "Hello" or greeting of some kind (in Vietnamese, of course) as was true of my experience in the United States and from every Vietnamese language tape or lesson I had learned. Stunned, I answered-asked, "Yes?" And in English, too! They laughed with hilarity. Even through my flushed embarrassed face, I felt the good-naturedness of it. After another exchange, the interviewing nun said, "We have to be quick to find the Vice Abbess because breakfast is ready to be served."

We raced off with a wave from the Abbess and, with luck, met the Vice Abbess just around the corner of the next building. The two teachers talked, and then the interviewing nun said, "The Vice Abbess asks, 'Do you know you have Buddha nature?'" This time, while still surprised, I was able to squeak out in English, "I know I'm *supposed* to know I have Buddha nature, but I don't know that I do." My sentence trailed off and my heart sank as I thought, "Damn, I just failed the tests! I won't be able to practice here now."

Meanwhile, the Vice Abbess laughed and clapped her hands together. The interviewing nun also laughed, and then they exchanged a few more words, too quick for me to understand. After that, the interviewing nun turned to me and said, "You're in! Let's get you to breakfast," as she grabbed my arm and rushed me off to join the other nuns heading for the guest house's dining hall.

○ ○ ○ ○

Since English is my second language, I've always been fascinated by the meaning of words. *Oppression* is the noun of *oppress*. It's from the Middle English *oppressen,* "to put pressure on," "crush," "burden," "overwhelm," which, from its Latin roots, means "to press on," "stifle," "overpower."[1]

As a Vietnamese American woman, these words really describe my experience. *Pressure. Crush. Burden. Overwhelm. Stifle. Overpower.* These words describe all systems of oppression. In terms of racism, for many of us Asian Americans and other people of color, if we are not diligent in noticing white supremacy culture's machinations, its impact on us, and how we can work with it, we can internalize it, believing that we are fragmented, even broken.

In the relative world, locations are specific and historical, bringing with them a need for definitions and labels as identifiers. And, with that, the whole range from negative to positive ideas grows from being named. We are all labeled. However, when located with numerous oppressive labels and their consequences, those in the down power are crushed, burdened, overwhelmed, stifled, and overpowered more and more with each label. We live in a world defined by ideas about self and others in ways that are driven by fears of differences and multiplicities, and thus, increasing isolation even more, fragmenting us from wholeness. Naming and being with the hurt and harm that's the impact of fear-based systems of oppression takes courage, hard work, and a framework that can support us to find new and appropriate meanings to our complex lives in the twenty-first century. The Engaged Four Noble Truths, reframing the ancient and fundamental wisdom of Buddhism, offers us the descriptions to inspire us *and* the skillful tools of the Engaged Eightfold Path to do so.

With these practices, we fully turn toward the hurt and harm that systems of domination and their machinations have caused to each of us and to the wholeness of life itself. We fully engage with the First Noble Truth to investigate how the social location imputed on us by white supremacy culture has hurt and harmed us, individually and collectively. From this starting point, we turn toward old dukkha, but this time—now—with Skillful View: the Engaged Four Noble Truths and its Eightfold Path.

○ ○ ○ ○

In the last chapter we discussed the three layers of absorption of the Engaged Four Noble Truths and the Engaged Eightfold Path and how they can be integrated through understanding, practice, and realizing.

We began by acknowledging that harm and harming are present. In doing so, we started to understand more fully the causes and conditions for how harm and harming came into being. In learning and practicing with the skillful means of the Engaged Eightfold Path, we realized we're becoming more confident that it is possible for us to have individual and collective agency to heal and restore from racialization and white supremacy culture. This process is about becoming more confident that Buddha nature is always present.

How can we build on this confidence from here on? The Three Refuges offer us the means to establish and sustain confidence in ourselves and the wholeness of our world.

With deeper practice, we start to see how the teachings of Buddhism are like a net themselves. Each set of teachings intertwine with others in various dimensional ways. As such, I'll put those three layers of absorption into another framework to show how the Three Refuges are also a way to see how practice is integrated. Begin by framing Understanding as *source,* Practice as *skillful means,* and Realization as *trust.*

THE THREE JEWELS

There is another description of jewels in Buddhism: The Three Jewels, also known as The Three Refuges. They are Buddha, Dharma, and Sangha. In the Soto Zen tradition, when we take our vows, we begin by taking refuge in The Three Jewels. To take refuge is to go to a haven where you can have a sense of confidence and trust that you will be seen as whole and complete. You are accepted and held. You are inseparable from the wholeness that is the net of life.

With refuge in The Three Jewels, our confidence in wholeness deepens. Without denying or invalidating our specificity or history, we begin to study how to turn it over in transcendent ways to promote individual and collective freedom.

Buddha

Buddha is a *source* of Understanding. He is an example that by simply being, we are whole. He is also an example for us of the possibility to be free of dukkha, harm, and harming. Buddha was a human being just like us and struggled, at times unskillfully, in thoughts, emotions, and actions, just like we have. Yet he wanted to find an explanation for how to meet hurt and harm, practice with it, and realize it. He and all buddha ancestors after him have done the same. By attaining enlightenment at the rising of the morning star, he showed that awakening is possible for all of us.

Thich Nhat Hanh, in *The Heart of the Buddha's Teaching*, writes:

> In Chinese and Vietnamese, practitioners always say, "I go back and rely on the Buddha in myself." Adding, "in myself" makes it clear that we ourselves are the Buddha. When we take refuge in Buddha, we must also understand, "The Buddha takes refuge in me." Without the second part, the first is not complete.[2]

If we are all Buddhas who don't know that we're Buddhas, then a source of our confidence can be ourselves, and also each other. Let us take confidence in ourselves and in each other that our capacity to know wholeness and be wholeness is always present when we meet each other in wholeness. This supports us to stay open to understanding each other.

Dharma

Dharma is *skillful means* of Practice. The Dharma is the teachings that Buddha and buddha ancestors have left us; not only in words and writings but in their examples. Reading this book and practicing the Dharma, the Engaged Four Noble Truths, and the Engaged Eightfold Path, gives us skillful means to connect and enact confidence that we can heal.

Not long ago, I received a call that the interview nun was coming to town with a few other nuns to deal with visas for travels to teach in Europe. In the years since our first meeting in Da Lat, she had been called to come serve a small community of Vietnamese American nuns not far from San Francisco. Hearing of their visit, as is a typical form of the practice of supporting monastics, I offered to take them to lunch. We had a lovely meal at a vegan Thai place, an introduction to Thai food for some of the nuns. During this time, I had to have translation of much of the conversations at the table of twelve of us. At the end, as we were saying our good-byes, one of the Vietnamese American nuns said to me, "You're a Twinkie, aren't you? You don't know Vietnamese."

The comment hit me hard. I had not seen it coming. Then, I remembered that even though it hurts to not be able to talk in my native language, I knew I had tried for many years in various ways. Therefore, while complex and layered, bringing hurt and pain at times, I also knew that "how Vietnamese I am" is not defined by how well I speak Vietnamese, nor by another. In that moment I had a choice to not take on any imputation.

It was a self-determined moment for how I can locate myself in wholeness. It was a moment in which I could clearly see how having the formulation and studies of the Engaged Four Noble Truths supported me to understand how both my and this nun's conditioning in individual and systemic contexts can bring about a result that had the potential to hurt and harm. And because of the years of having practiced the Engaged Eightfold Path, factors that also offered grounding and liberatory awareness thus allowed me to know I have the agency to choose a response from understanding and compassion instead of old reactivity. I remembered that it's the net where life energy is, that *the wholeness of everything* was the source for healing, restoration, and well-being. In any moment, I am part of wholeness and thus I have agency to accept, reject, or, as in that moment, not be bound by causes and conditions—old or present, expected or unexpected—that defined me. Such moments strengthen my trust and faith in practice.

I hope that your studies and practice with the teachings in these pages can offer you a reminder also that you are more than any one definition, imputed on us by another or by systems of oppression. Learning to trust this knowledge is the work, and the results, of our practice with the Engaged Eightfold Path—by itself and as applied to racialization and white supremacy culture's racism and other forms of domination.

Sangha

Sangha is *trust*, which is required for Realization. Sangha is us, in community, practicing being and enacting wholeness together. "Trust" is difficult for many of us. For me, trust is the result of strengthened confidence. Every time you read something in these pages, and it resonates with you, and you nod to yourself, that's an affirmation that you are building confidence in the teachings and in yourself. When another person in the world does the same, then already there is a connection, even though it may not be evident. Each of our nods is like sending out a thread to strengthen the net of wholeness that's always here but that we can forget is supporting and connecting us. When you engage in any of the practices offered, and when you try it out in interactions with another being or in areas of your life, confidence builds.

Sangha is where we practice and will likely rub against each other, especially when conditions are challenging. As we endeavor to skillfully practice with the Engaged Eightfold Path, healing and restoration are possible, giving us confidence that the bonds between us are strong. Trust comes when we gain confidence in the bonds between source and practice, and between us and with the net, realizing wholeness.

Buddha as a source example of how to awaken to understanding wholeness.

Dharma provides skillful means to practice confidently connecting and enacting wholeness.

Sangha offers us ways to realize trusting in wholeness, individually and collectively.

○ ○ ○ ○

In Soto Zen, there is a tradition called Way-Seeking Mind talks. Each person shares how they came to Buddhist practice, often as a way to introduce themselves to the sangha or community of practitioners. Generally, most people start by sharing their family background, birth order, and what their parents did, where they've lived, and if any, religious or spiritual upbringing. Often, there's a story that is the pivotal point for the why or the what that brings them to Buddhist practice. In the main Zen lineage I've practiced in, a person can be asked to give more than one talk because they have moved to the different practice communities within the lineage, and also when they are the Shuso, the Head Monk—a position when your teacher feels you are ready to teach and so mentors your teaching during one three-month practice period.

It has been useful to have given several of these Way-Seeking Mind talks throughout my more than twenty years of Soto Zen practice. Each time, it has been an opportunity to reexamine how I've made sense of my life. In particular, how I've suffered, how I've worked with it, and how, with practice, I am suffering less now. Writing this book feels like it's been a form of giving my Way-Seeking Mind talk. Reflecting back to the opening story in this book with Sekkei Harada Roshi: I, like the Buddha and ancestors, have looked for ways to make sense of my suffering. In "knowing dukkha [hurt and harm] completely" with the descriptions and methods of the Engaged Eightfold Path, we give ourselves the opportunity to *understand its impacts **and** activate our agency to choose how it is relevant* in our lives *now*.

In doing so, we become more confident in the Third Noble Truth: the alleviation and ending of dukkha is possible.

As set out in the Introduction, we've traveled the Path together in what I termed the three essential aspects of healing from systems of domination such as white supremacy culture's racism: acknowledging its impact, both individually and systemically; knowing what shifts are especially needed to heal and restore from it; and learning how to put those shifts into practice. As you have read through this book and engaged with the Practice

Pauses, I hope you have gained confidence in the Third Noble Truth as you journey to healing from white supremacy culture's racism or other oppressive forces.

○ ○ ○ ○

The majority of people in the convert Buddhist settings come to practice thinking that its main aim is to give them access to a calm and quiet mind. Buddhist practices can certainly provide us access to knowing and being in these qualities. However, as I see it, as our practice matures, it's actually about gaining confidence in the Third Noble Truth's message that the end of dukkha is possible. And as our confidence strengthens, it is actually joy that arises. As stated before, I've framed mudita, the third of the four Brahma Viharas, as inclusive joy: the joy when we experience belonging to the wholeness of life, to all aspects of the Net of Indra.

As such, I would like to offer this meditation on mudita.

PRACTICE PAUSE

Mudita/Inclusive Joy Meditation

As is reflective of its emphasis on inclusiveness, mudita's meditation begins by offering joy to others first, classically in this order: mentor or good friend, neutral person, challenging person, self, and then all beings.

As you've done other Brahma Viharas in this book, the setup instructions will be brief, and then I'll offer the phrases in the "plural you" format to echo mudita's inclusivity. Change the pronouns to fit when doing the other categories:

- First, take an easeful posture.

- Close your eyes if you would like.

- Remember, there's no need to "push through" at any point, and some find it useful to connect to the intentions of this meditation by touching their heart-space.

- Say the following phrases silently or quietly out loud to yourself. In between each phrase, be sure to pause and feel how it "lands" for you; that is, rest in the result of cultivating each of these qualities as you say them:

  May we know success is when we've given our best effort.

  Let us know and enjoy good fortune and success right here and right now, however it's coming up.

  May we connect to the confidence that suffering and the causes of suffering can end.

  Let us know satisfaction and contentment here and now.

  May we be able to *connect* in the joy of knowing we're all part of wholeness.

- Now take a deep breath, and on the exhale, just let yourself feel joy, and then rest in that. Then rest in the sense of its completeness: the fullness and wholeness of its essence.

- Then radiate it toward (the category) you're practicing with.

- In the "all beings" category, feel it coming back to you, as you are included in this category.

- Feel and rest in the inclusivity of joy.

"Do you know you have Buddha nature?"

We *begin* in wholeness. We are never separate from it. We just don't know it because conditioning gets in the way. Our conditioning can create unwise attention and harmful actions that take us away from knowing the true nature of life, which is that each of us are beings *of* wholeness—you are an indivisible part of the wholeness of the net that supports this life we are all *in* together.

Thus, we practice to "come home" to the home that's already here.

My *honshi,* root teacher, Zenkei Blanche Hartman, tells a story about her first experience with Zen practice:

In my first zazen instruction, Katagiri Dainin Roshi said, "We sit to settle the self on the self and let the flower of our life force bloom," again suggesting that everything we need is right here.[3]

This is beautiful and aspirational, and yet white supremacy culture's machination makes this knowledge difficult for all who are impacted by racism, and much more for Asian Americans and other people of color. So much of the suffering inside me and in the world stems from the inability to be fully alive, to stay connected to this very moment, to be able to experience its blooming. This includes staying connected to the sorrows *and* difficulties that are inherent in our conditioned life. We cannot escape the unconsciousness that each of us has, individually, collectively, and societally. What we can do as a response based in wholeness is to *not* close our eyes to the suffering, the harm, and harming of our past and its results in the present.

In Thailand there is a practice in which one purchases a buddha statue and then takes it to an *arhat,* an enlightened person, for them to open the statue's eyes. Similarly, what we practice is to open our own eyes, to not turn away from our own suffering and the suffering of the world. Each time we gain experiential knowledge that we *can* do it, in small or large ways, our confidence grows in our capacity and ability to fully live life in all conditions. In the midst of our suffering, we can connect to our capacity for freedom, which comes from yoniso manasikara, "attention that takes the whole into account." How to know and live from it while making it possible for others is the heart of bodhisattva practice.

A bodhisattva is one who lives fully knowing and engaging in all of life, nothing left out, all inclusive. In Mahayana Buddhism, which Zen is part of, a bodhisattva is one who lives knowing this and yet will not become self-enlightened; instead, they aim to spread this knowledge and practices to all beings. Thus, even if suffering, such as racism, is extreme in life, enlightenment is present and shines in, through, and between us. We will not be destroyed by it if we are able to use it to heal ourselves, each other, and the world. To do so, we practice to remember, and at times, to reclaim our confidence in the knowledge that we are never separate from wholeness.

This is the gift of the Engaged Four Noble Truths: By turning toward dukkha, hurt, and harm with skillful means through the study, practice, and realization of the Engaged Eightfold Path, we learn to redirect our conditioned thinking into wholeness thinking. From wholeness thinking, its associative beliefs and actions based on connection, inclusivity, kindness, and nonharming blooms. We can live in this way with compassion and confidence, knowing we are not alone because we are part of the net, part of the fabric of life itself.

We are taught a version of the world. As we practice, the experience and wisdom we learn, along with the strengthening of kindness, compassion, inclusive joy, and equanimity, gives us the opportunity to reframe our vision of what the world is and how we can cocreate it.

Practicing with the Engaged Four Noble Truths, and its Engaged Eightfold Path, has helped me to see the wholeness of the world and my place in it. May it do the same for you.

Home is here.

May this be for the benefit of all beings.

ACKNOWLEDGMENTS

IN WHOLENESS WE ARE NEVER ALONE. In wholeness nothing is "mine" alone. In wholeness, there's a net which connects all.

This book came into being out of causes and conditions. So many seeds bloomed out of an endless network of validation, support, and resonance.

The "in-joke" on the Way-Seeking Mind talk is that your mind has always been *in* the Way. To a certain extent, we practice to realize that what we seek has always been present. You have never been far from the Way. You and it have been here all the time, intertwined.

As such, another way to understand what a Way-Seeking Mind talk can be is that it's an opportunity to realize we inter-are with wholeness; that, indeed, we have never been anywhere except in wholeness. A form of realizing this is to see how I have arrived here through a network of support and guidance.

In Buddhism, the foremost and enduring supports are The Three Jewels: Buddha, Dharma, and Sangha.

I want to thank Buddha for finding out and then putting forth these teachings. The ancestors for transmitting such transformative, liberatory wisdom, on and on, further exemplifying the teachings. In this regard, I thank the Japanese American Sokoji sangha for sponsoring Reverend Shunryu Suzuki to San Francisco in 1959. Thank you to my ordination and Dharma Transmission Root Teacher, Zenkei Blanche Hartman Daiosho, for her love, patience, humanness, and joyful pride in my sharing of the Dharma. After her death, it has been through the enduring gentle compassion and guidance from my current teachers, Shosan Victoria Austin and Gil Fronsdal, that my practice and many of the ideas and articulations in this book have come into fruition. Nine full prostrations to you both, over and over again.

These other exemplary teachers have also been a support to my practice through their teachings and presence:

Thich Nhat Hanh, of course, is considered the originator of the term *engaged Buddhism,* setting an example and making it a definitive part of Buddhist practice. Reading Sister Chan Khong's autobiography, *Learning True Love: Practicing in the Time of War* (Parallax Press, 1993), on hers and his work developing engaged Buddhism with youths in Vietnam, opened me to the possibilities of the wholeness of Buddhism as practice not separate from social justice work. Dare I say that my development of the Engaged Four Noble Truths as shared in this book is but a strand in this ongoing work to formulate ways in which the ancient teachings continue to be applicable in our current times. Just as when I practiced with both of them mindful walking and doing the Touching the Earth prostrations on the undulating hills of a retreat center in Northern California in the mid-1990s, I sense the reclamation of "home" reverberating in our practices and teachings.

Practicing overseas in Asia brought a resonance through my body and spirit that echoes still. My endless gratitude to Sekkei Harada Roshi and the Hosshinji staff and sangha for showing me the root of Soto Zen practice and access to emptiness. My travels and practice with Arahant Luang Pu Punalit and the many Thai and non-Thai practitioners were where I truly learned the depth of devotion and the wordlessness of being fully seen and known. To Ni Su Thuan Tue and the other teachers and sisters of the Truc Lam, Bamboo Forest, Nunnery in Vietnam, this "longest foreigner practicing with us" is grateful for having grounded myself in the soil of practice with you there in Da Lat, the hometown of my birth parents.

If these pages have brought relief or an end to your dukkha, it is due to these many teachers. Any mistakes in the Dharma or otherwise are mine and mine alone.

I also want to thank my ancestors, known and unknown. Known, first and foremost to my birth mother, Nguyen Thi Bac Tuyet, wherever and whatever you are now, may you know your life and suffering has not been in vain. All that I am is because of your gentleness, loving presence, and sacrifices. I want to thank my birth sister Mai Kha for having traveled this life with me. I've survived in part due to your unfaltering caring. To John Paul, your sincere brotherly love sustains me. To Betty and Merrill Shutt and the extended family I gained when adopted, I'm so grateful for your openness of hearts and homes to me and all the iterations of "self"s I've exhibited throughout the years. Not all were pretty to be sure. Gayle, Sue, Eric, Alex, Andrew, Lucas, Galen, and Kylei, our love and care for each other grows and strengthens with time (especially as we approach fifty years since adoption!).

My gratitude to my chosen Vietnamese American family: Bac Lieng Tran, Em Ryan Nguyen, Em Anais Nguyen, and Anh Chinh Nguyen. Thank you for accepting me fully as I am and supporting both my practices in Vietnamese-ness and the Dharma! From you all and your love, healing continues to bloom.

I thank the Dharma for having never left me. From my deluded view, it truly is a gift to come home here.

As Dharma is also Nature, I'm forever indebted to the Russian River and the redwoods here, along with all its plethora of wildlife (spiders, pappi, and water plants, oh my!). Thank you for your support and nourishment. There have been many hours of resting in overflowing gratitude for the beauty and awe-ness you've revealed to this humble being.

Sangha: To know that I am supported by all beings is a realization beyond words. And while I foolishly try to name a few here, please see them as both jewels and net.

Home Is Here was an arising from years of organizing, practice groups, retreats, and writings that began in the mid-1990s, with the formulation of the Buddhists of Color, Women of Color, and People of Color groups that I was a part of in the San Francisco Bay Area. I want to thank Marlene Jones, Margarita Loinaz, and Ryumon Gutierrez Baldoquin for being my first practice teachers and mentors of racially affirming and freeing practices and sanghas. Deep love and hugs to Jessica Tan and Lauren Leslie, the main caretakers with me of the Buddhists of Color. Who knew that our main aim of "just holding space" in an ecumenical-Buddhist way for all was a seed that has sprouted this? In 2000, many of us from these groups and others, of all races, working on racial diversity and equity in convert Buddhism in the San Francisco Bay Area, were part of the publication of *Making the Invisible Visible: Healing Racism in Our Sanghas*. In the same year, the Buddhist Peace Fellowship, with its long history of dedication to addressing racism and concerns of various ethnic groups in U.S. Buddhism, came out with an issue devoted to Buddhists of Asian Descent in the United States in its quarterly magazine *Turning Wheel, the Journal of Socially Engaged Buddhism*. That issue was edited by Mushim Ikeda. Mushim, along with Larry Yang and I, have been traveling on the Path in the Bay Area for many years, our ways separating and then coming back together, but always with the aim of anti-oppression and in the spirit of wholeness. Thank you to you both for your *kalyanamitra*, spiritual friendship, and guidance all these years.

I also want to thank the Hemera Foundation for their firm support from the very beginning of the development of these Engaged Four Noble Truths. Their support was not only to me but to the numerous students who have benefitted from their funding of scholarships to the majority of the iterations of Lotus Rising from Mud (Lotus) and The Dharma of Being Antiracist (DBA) courses. In many ways, the caring staff of Hemera were like copartners in my response to the need for *Home Is Here,* as they, hearing the request, made it possible for me to have the means to find ways to produce this manuscript.

To my teacher friends Reverend Dana Takagi, bruni davila, and Ayya Dhammadipa, thank you for the Dharma, cultural, and social justice discussions, feedback, and encouragements during all the turns and twists as these teachings were being developed. Many a time, your bodhisattva responses to my calls for help and support enriched not only the outcomes but, at times, most importantly, the process!

Helping me to make the Engaged Four Noble Truths and its Engaged Eightfold Path more than just theory are the coteachers of the different versions of The Dharma of Being Antiracist. Thank you Reverend Sarah Dojin Emerson for being open to that "Who is 'we'?" conversation that led us, with Reverend Charlie Korin Pokorny, to work together to further formulate how to use the Engaged Four Noble Truths to actualize and sustain antiracist sanghas. Then with the murder of George Floyd, the three of us responding together with Dalila Bothwell, and later with Dawn Haney and Linda Gonzalez, to teaching The Dharma of Being Antiracist courses. Deep appreciation for you all in making the Engaged Four Noble Truths applicable and meaningful to the numerous locations in systems of oppression we addressed implicitly and explicitly.

To the many Asian American students who bravely asked for help and support from the latest racially imputed harm brought on us by others at the beginning of COVID-19, know that your requests have opened the way for the many others wanting a Dharma that mirrors, validates, and values us and our experiences on and off the cushion.

All the students of all races and social locations who have wholeheartedly and courageously met the impacts of white supremacy culture on you, know that your sweat-and-tears participations in these two courses have verified that the Dharma can and does heal and restore us to wholeness, individually and collectively.

I want to thank Chenxing Han for her presence and book *Be the Refuge: Raising the Voices of Asian American Buddhists.* The book was a timely balm to the suffering of racism toward all Asian and Asian American practitioners, bringing attention in particular to our invisibilization and minimization. *Home Is Here* started out as a response to the call for a more appropriately contextual text to the Lotus Rising from Mud and The Dharma of Being Antiracist courses. Your voice and that book inspired me to begin to conceive that my truths could be skillful means to expressions of the Dharma that would be needed, heard, and valued.

Thank you to Kate Goka, one of the first students who helped with the initial chapters' drafts of *Home Is Here,* supporting and nudging me to expand and clarify the teachings, my voice, and scope.

Endless thanks to Ellin O'Leary for her unfaltering cheerleading; walks-and-talks through the redwoods; offerings of foods at my doorstep, reminding me of the ancient practice of alms-giving to monastics, during the many months of manuscript manipulations; and for her keen editing.

Development editor Amy Reed gave structure and order and shored up the "house" that is *Home Is Here,* while also echoing its healing value and need as restoration from her resonating locations. Eunji Nancy Son, associate editor, was buddha-sent, bringing her years of Zen practice and Korean American view and heart to flesh out the manuscript in germane ways. *Home Is Here* is better for having had these editors' eyes and hearts on it.

Thank you to Gillian Hamel of North Atlantic Books for their initial and continuing enthusiasm for *Home Is Here.* Their gentle patience and care for the manuscript is echoed by all the NAB staff I interacted with. I'm so glad you all saw the value of the book and made it available to others.

Thank you to Tamaron Greene for your keen eyes, honed by experience, in helping this book be a labor of love that's also grounded in pragmatism.

A deep, deep bow of thanks to Shinsen Lynn Eubanks for her generosity of spirit and practice, making her house on the banks of the Russian River available for this endeavor. What started out as a six-week "writing retreat" became almost a year! Her devotion to the Dharma and this iteration of it is beyond bounds. May you know that healing and restoration from this book is part of the echo of the Buddha nature of these surroundings, and your generosity in sharing it.

For all the students of Access to Zen Sangha, my gratitude to you for your eagerness for the Dharma, devotion to its expression through me and our interactions with each other and the world, and support to make A2Z truly an inclusive, anti-oppression sangha. Because of you all, the teachings flow.

Finally, though endlessly, my gratitude goes to my life partner, Deb Svoboda. I thank you for your deep love and tender care for me as part of the animal phylum. Your insightful MacGyver mind and skills amaze me every day as your deep, unconditionally kind presence graces my world and is an inspiration for me to be the best person for you and everyone else. In particular, thank you for your generosity and patience during the many months as I "retreated" to write this book.

As you can see, there is no "me" who wrote this book because it came out of response and has been supported throughout space and time, and thus "here" all along. This Way-Seeking Mind book has been realized.

Thank you, readers, for being a part of it.

All of us, together, are home in this net of wholeness.

Rev. Liên Shutt
Russian River
Graton Rancheria territory
December 2022

APPENDIX
Practice Pauses

Chapter 1: The Engaged Four Noble Truths

Chapter 2: Skillful View

Chapter 3: Skillful Concentration

Chapter 4: Skillful Motivation

Chapter 5: Skillful Effort

NOTES

INTRODUCTION

1 Patricia Hill Collins, *Black Feminist Thought: Knowledge, Consciousness, and the Politics of Empowerment* (New York: Routledge, 2009).

CHAPTER 1

1 Gil Fronsdal, author, teacher, and Buddhist scholar. Personal discussion with the author, July 2022.

CHAPTER 2

1 California State Legislature, "Foreign Miner's License," American Social History Project, Resources for Teachers, n.d., www.shec.ashp.cuny .edu/items/show/1714.

2 PBS, "Chinese Immigrants and the Gold Rush," *American Experience,* n.d., www.pbs.org/wgbh/americanexperience/features/goldrush-chinese -immigrants/.

3 John Johnson Jr., "How Los Angeles Covered Up the Massacre of 17 Chinese," *LA Weekly,* March 10, 2011, www.laweekly.com/how-los-angeles -covered-up-the-massacre-of-17-chinese/.

4 Erika Lee, *The Making of Asian America: A History,* (New York: Simon & Schuster, 2015), 67.

5 Karen Grigsby Bates, "How Vincent Chin's Death Gave Others a Voice," NPR Code Switch, March 27, 2021, www.npr.org/sections /codeswitch/2021/03/27/981718272/how-vincent-chins-death-gave -others-a-voice.

6 The Pluralism Project, "Buddhists in the American West," Harvard University, 2020, https://pluralism.org/buddhists-in-the-american-west.

CHAPTER 3

1 Thomas Cleary and J. C. Cleary, trans., *The Blue Cliff Record* (Boulder, CO: Shambhala, 1977), 309.
2 Chenxing Han, *Be the Refuge: Raising the Voices of Asian American Buddhists* (Berkeley, CA: North Atlantic Books, 2021), 10.
3 As quoted in Chenxing Han, *Be the Refuge,* 21–24.
4 Aaron J. Lee, *Angry Asian Buddhist* (blog), 2007–2017, www.angryasian buddhist.com.
5 Marlene Lenthang, "Atlanta Shooting and the Legacy of Misogyny and Racism Against Asian Women," ABC News, March 21, 2021, www.abcnews.go.com/US/atlanta-shooting-legacy-misogyny-racism -asian-women/story?id=76533776.
6 May We Gather, www.maywegather.org/49-days.

CHAPTER 4

1 Merriam-Webster.com, s.v. "stereotype."

CHAPTER 5

1 Shunryu Suzuki, "June 1, 1969," https://shunryu12.rssing.com /chan-50790865/article6.html.
2 Gil Fronsdal, "The Five Hindrances: Introduction," Audio Dharma, October 13, 2008, www.audiodharma.org/talks/1399.
3 Robin DiAngelo, "White Fragility," *International Journal of Critical Pedagogy* 3:3 (2011), 54–70, https://libjournal.uncg.edu/ijcp/article /viewFile/249/116.
4 Blanche Hartman, *Seeds for a Boundless Life: Zen Teachings from the Heart* (Boston: Shambhala, 2015), 10.
5 Louis Noe-Bustamente, Neil G. Ruiz, Mark Hugo Lopez, and Khadijah Edwards, "About a Third of Asian Americans Say They Have Changed Their Daily Routine Due to Concerns Over Threats, Attacks," Pew

Research Center, May 9, 2022, www.pewresearch.org/fact-tank/2022/05/09/about-a-third-of-asian-americans-say-they-have-changed-their-daily-routine-due-to-concerns-over-threats-attacks/.

CHAPTER 6

1 Eihei Dogen, *The Wholehearted Way: A Translation of Eihei Dogen's Bendowa with Commentary by Kosho Uchiyama Roshi,* trans. Shohaku Okumura and Taigen Daniel Leighton (Rutland, VT: Tuttle, 1997), 30.
2 Cathy Park Hong, *Minor Feelings: An Asian American Reckoning* (New York: One World, 2020), 87.
3 W. E. B. Dubois, *The Souls of Black Folk: Essays and Sketches* (Chicago: A. C. McClurg, 1903), repr. Project Gutenberg, www.gutenberg.org/files/408/408-h/408-h.htm.
4 Cathy Park Hong, *Minor Feelings,* 86.
5 History.com, "Manifest Destiny," A&E Television Networks, November 15, 2019, www.history.com/topics/westward-expansion/manifest-destiny.

CHAPTER 7

1 Meryl Kornfield and Hannah Knowles, "Captain Who Said Spa Shooting Suspect Had 'Bad Day' No Longer a Spokesman on Case, Official Says," *Washington Post,* March 18, 2021, www.washingtonpost.com/nation/2021/03/17/jay-baker-bad-day/.
2 Naina Bajekal, "The 10 Cities with the Highest LGBT Percentage in the U.S.," *Time,* March 20, 2015, www.time.com/3752220/lgbt-san-francisco/.
3 Erika Lee, *The Making of Asian America: A History* (New York: Simon & Schuster, 2015), 304.
4 Christina B. Hanhardt, "Queer History," The American Historian, Organization of American Historians, 2019, www.oah.org/tah/issues/2019/may/queer-history/.
5 "Upaddha Sutta: Half (of the Holy Life)" (SN 45.2), trans. Thanissaro Bhikkhu, Access to Insight, 1997, www.accesstoinsight.org/tipitaka/sn/sn45/sn45.002.than.html.

CHAPTER 8

1 Michelle Kretzer, "What You Can Do Right Now to Save Bees," PETA, August 17, 2017, www.peta.org/living/food/whats-killing-bees-how -to-save-the-honey-bees/.

2 Michelle Getchell, "Manifest Destiny," Khan Academy, n.d., www .khanacademy.org/humanities/us-history/the-early-republic/age-of -jackson/a/manifest-destiny.

3 Blanche Hartman, "The Old Woman Burns Down the Hermitage," in *The Hidden Lamp: Stories from Twenty-Five Centuries of Awakened Women,* eds. Florence Caplow and Susan Moon (Boston: Wisdom Publications, 2013), 103.

CHAPTER 9

1 Kazuaki Tanahashi, *Treasury of the True Dharma Eye: Zen Master Dogen's Shōbō Genzo* (Boston: Shambhala, 2013), 29.

2 bell hooks, "Contemplation and Transformation," in *Buddhist Women on the Edge: Contemporary Perspectives from the Western Frontier,* ed. Marianne Dresser (Berkeley, CA: North Atlantic Books, 1996), 291.

CONCLUSION

1 Merriam-Webster.com, s.v. "oppress."

2 Thich Nhat Hanh, *Heart of the Buddha's Teaching: Transforming Suffering into Peace, Joy, and Liberation* (New York: Broadway Books, 1999), 162.

3 Blanche Hartman, "Just to Be Alive is Enough," Lion's Roar, June 4, 2021, www.lionsroar.com/just-to-be-alive-is-enough/.